Pat Hancock

THE BIG BOOK OF

Crazy Canadian Trivia

Previously published as *Crazy Canadian Trivia*,
Crazy Canadian Trivia 2, *Crazy Canadian Trivia 3*
and *Crazy Canadian Trivia 4*

Cover illustration by Bill Dickson

Interior illustrations by
Bill Dickson and Dimitri Kostic

Scholastic Canada Ltd.
Toronto New York London Auckland Sydney
Mexico City New Delhi Hong Kong Buenos Aires

Scholastic Canada Ltd.
604 King Street West, Toronto, Ontario M5V 1E1, Canada

Scholastic Inc.
557 Broadway, New York, NY 10012, USA

Scholastic Australia Pty Limited
PO Box 579, Gosford, NSW 2250, Australia

Scholastic New Zealand Limited
Private Bag 94407, Greenmount, Auckland, New Zealand

Scholastic Children's Books
Euston House, 24 Eversholt Street, London NW1 1DB, UK

The following trademarked names have been used in this book:
Balderdash, Band-Aid, Bubblicious, Crispy Crunch, DOUBLEMINT, JUICY FRUIT,
Mind Trap, Nike, Pictionary, A Question of Scruples, Pogo, Scrabble, Ski-doo,
Tickle Me Elmo, Tilley Hat, Trivial Pursuit, Zamboni.

Library and Archives Canada Cataloguing in Publication

Hancock, Pat, author The big book of crazy Canadian trivia / by Pat Hancock;
illustrated by Bill Dickson and Dimitri Kostic.

ISBN 978-1-4431-2831-5

1. Canada–Miscellanea–Juvenile literature. I. Dickson, Bill, illustrator
II. Kostic, Dimitri, illustrator III. Title.

FC58.H27 2014   j971.002   C2013-905965-2
                                                             C2013-905966-0

6 5 4 3 2 1   Printed in Canada 139   14 15 16 17 18 19

Introduction

Whenever I come across an amazing, wonderful, wild or wacky fact — especially one about Canada or Canadians — I can't resist the urge to share it with someone. That's why I was so happy to have the chance to write the four *Crazy Canadian Trivia* books. I could say, "Wow!" "Incredible!" "Did you know?" and "Listen to this!" to thousands of people.

Now you have the chance to snack on the tastiest trivia tidbits from all those books in *The Big Book of Crazy Canadian Trivia*. As you sample the offerings in this colossal collection, don't be surprised to find yourself saying, "Wow! Listen to this!" I should know — the urge to share crazy Canadian trivia is irresistible.

Pat Hancock

The Strongest Man in the World

Louis Cyr was born on October 10, 1863, in a little town near Montreal, Saint-Cyprien-de-Napierville. He was a big baby — around 8 kilograms at birth — and he grew up to be a big, powerful, 135-kilogram man. His 61-centimetre biceps were the size of some women's waists, and his 91-centimetre thighs were bigger than the waists of many men.

After he won competitions to determine the strongest man in the United States, and then in Canada, Cyr's fame as the Canadian Hercules began to spread. In his twenties and early thirties he won every strongman and weightlifting competition in Canada and the United States. When he went to London, England, in 1892 and lifted 1652 kilograms on his back and 250 kilograms with one finger, everyone agreed that he was indeed the strongest man in the world.

Funny Money

For nearly 80 years, starting in 1685, playing cards were as good as gold in Canada. During that time, they were used like money in New France, France's colony in North America back then.

When real money was in short supply, the governor would have some playing cards cut into quarters, and assign each part a value equal to a certain number of French coins. To make them official, the cards were marked with the treasurer's wax seal, and signed by the governor and his intendant or business manager.

When supply ships finally arrived from France with money from the king or from the sale of furs sent back to Europe the year before, people could cash in their card money for the real thing.

The Buck Stopped Here

And speaking of money, it was a chemistry professor working at Montreal's McGill University who came up with the ink the United States chose to print their money with, from 1862 onward. Professor Thomas Sterry Hunt's special green ink couldn't be reproduced by photography, making it almost impossible for forgers to churn out fake "greenbacks," the nickname given to American bills.

Ice Cream, Anyone?

July 24, 1988, wasn't just another workday for the folks at Palm Dairy in Edmonton, Alberta. Under the watchful eye of supervisor Mike Rogiani they shovelled and shaped 20 313 kilograms of ice cream into a huge mound. Then they ladled on 4404 kilos of syrup, followed by 244 kilos of toppings. *Voilà* — the world's biggest sundae!

. . . that tornadoes in Canada have been known to strip the feathers right off chickens running around the barnyard?

Highest High Tide

The Bay of Fundy, between New Brunswick and southwest Nova Scotia, has the largest tides in the world. High tide at the head of the bay can reach heights of up to 16 metres! The surging ebb and flow of the ocean in this part of the world is also what causes an impressive natural phenomenon — the reversing falls on the Saint John River, near Saint John, New Brunswick. When the tide is going out, water flows over a rock shelf near the river's mouth and out into the sea. But as the tide comes in, the level of the river rises to the point where water starts spilling over the shelf back into the river, in effect changing the direction of the waterfall.

The Greatest Athletes in Their Field

Two members of the Canadian Sports Hall of Fame aren't people, but horses. Northern Dancer, the greatest Canadian racehorse ever, was named to the Hall in 1965. He sired more than 1000 foals. Some people believe that his lineage will result in more champions than any horse that ever lived.

World champion show jumper Big Ben and his human partner Ian Millar both became Hall of Famers in 1996.

Two boats are also members of the Hall of Fame — the *Bluenose and Miss Supertest III*. The *Bluenose*, the elegant schooner pictured on the Canadian dime and on the stamp below, was one of the greatest sailing ships ever built. From 1921 to 1938 she was also the fastest, winning every sailing race she entered. She and her winning captain, Angus Walters, were made members of the Hall of Fame in 1955.

Miss Supertest III was a world champion speedboat. She and her pilot, Robert Hayward, ruled the world hydroplane racing circuit from 1959 to 1961, and entered the Hall in 1960.

A Secret Life

When Leslie McFarlane died in 1977, one newspaper article remembered him as Canada's best-selling author ever. That came as a surprise to a lot of people. McFarlane had been a well respected and successful writer, playwright, scriptwriter and film director — but best-selling novelist hadn't been his claim to fame. That's because until he wrote his autobiography in 1976, no one knew that he had written nearly two dozen of the most popular American adventure stories for boys.

In his autobiography, McFarlane revealed that he was Franklin W. Dixon, the author of the Hardy Boys series. He wrote the series for Edward L. Stratemeyer, a hugely successful American publisher, himself a series writer for younger readers. Stratemeyer paid McFarlane a small fee for each story, rather than giving him a percentage from each book sold, and made him promise not to tell anyone that he was Franklin W. Dixon. That's why no one knew that McFarlane's books had sold over 12 million copies — not even his own children! He had kept his secret for nearly 50 years.

Some wilderness hikers like to use pack animals — horses, donkeys, mules or even llamas — to carry their gear. But whichever animals they use, they need to make sure to pack food for them as well as for themselves, if they're trekking through one of Canada's national parks. Without food, the animals might start nibbling on the park's grass. And that's a no-no. Hikers will be fined unless they can produce a special permit that allows the animals to graze.

Colour-Coded Critters

If you're in Toronto or Montreal, check out the squirrels that live there. Most of the squirrels in Montreal are grey, whereas 80 per cent of Toronto's are black. And in Exeter, Ontario, these frisky cousins of the rat are all white. Go figure.

Caddy for Hire

For five years after it opened in 1997, the nine-hole River Valley Golf and Country Club near Stratford, Ontario, had some super-strong caddies. They were llamas, South American members of the camel family that look a lot like dromedaries, but without a hump.

The llamas were a big hit with golfers. They could carry two sets of golf clubs without working up a sweat. But they wouldn't put up with being overloaded. Pile too much on them and they'd just sit down and refuse to budge.

MOVING DAY

While most other Canadians are enjoying the July 1 Canada Day holiday, nearly 200 000 renters in Montreal are caught up in moving-day madness. Most apartment leases expire on June 30, leaving tenants scrambling to shift their furniture and belongings from one place to the next all at the same time.

Trucks and moving vans have to be booked months in advance, often at hourly rates three to four times higher than usual. And even if you're lucky enough to rent one of those vehicles, you still have to figure out ways to get your furniture down the stairs while two or three other tenants are trying to get theirs up. People pile their stuff on lawns and sidewalks, waiting for old tenants to move out. Rain can turn the entire process into an even bigger nightmare than it already is.

A Deep-Sea Giant

The Pacific waters off the coast of British Columbia are home to the world's largest species of octopus, *Octopus dofleini*. This eight-armed monster of the deep can grow up to 9 metres wide and weigh more than 100 kilograms. Tinted a dark red, it can change colour to blend in with its surroundings, and if it loses one of its arms, it can grow it back. Like other octopi, it squirts out dark ink when it's being threatened so that it can make a quick escape under cover of the darkness.

Researchers who have studied these creatures think that they're very smart and can teach each other what they've learned. Thank goodness they haven't learned to slip aboard boats and hitch a ride. Yet.

Ladies and Gentlemen, Start Your Bathtubs!

Nanaimo, British Columbia, is the second largest city on Vancouver Island. It's separated from the mainland by the Strait of Georgia. On the third Sunday in July each year, thousands of spectators head across that strait to take in one of the wackiest water races in the world — the Nanaimo International Bathtub Race. Originally a 1967 Centennial celebration involving only real old-fashioned bathtubs, the race now attracts some pretty amazing watercraft made out of fibreglass. But no matter what they're made of they still must look like your basic, roll-edged bathtub with a motor on one end. And no souped-up engines are allowed. Members of the Loyal Nanaimo Bathtub Society make sure of that.

Sweet
City
Square

Nanaimo also lays claim to another international success — the melt-in-your-mouth chocolate treat that bears its name. Rumours abound about where the layered square got its start, or what it was called originally, but there's no doubt about which place has adopted it and given it a permanent home. City officials give visitors a best-ever recipe for Nanaimo Bars, and the city's unofficial mascot is — you guessed it — a walking, talking Nanaimo Bar named Nanaimo Barney.

Apparently, one or two recipes for Nanaimo Bar look-alikes did appear in British and American cookbooks early on, but there's no doubt that another sweet treat is strictly Canadian. Gooey-delicious raisin-filled butter tarts were born in the kitchens of Canadian pioneer families. Mmmmmmm-good for them.

DID YOU KNOW... . . . that the St. John's Regatta — a series of boat races held annually in Newfoundland — is the longest-running sporting event in North America? The regatta was first held in 1818.

Storm of the Century

A six-day ice storm mercilessly battered eastern Ontario, Quebec and the Maritimes from January 4 to 10 in 1998. Weighed down under layers of ice as thick as 8 centimetres, millions of trees splintered like toothpicks and thousands of kilometres of power lines snapped like over-stretched guitar strings. The storm did at least $500 million of damage and left 1 673 000 customers without electricity, nearly 1 400 000 of those in Quebec alone.

Sap It Up

Many of the trees damaged during the 1998 Quebec ice storm were maples, putting a dent in the country's annual maple syrup production. Quebec produces 90 per cent of this traditionally Canadian syrup. It takes 40 litres of sap to boil up 1 litre of the genuine article. Fake maple syrup is just plain glucose with artificial flavouring. Quebeckers have a name for such a pitiful pretender. They call it *sirop de poteau* — telephone-pole or dead-tree syrup.

In June, 1988, folks in Lefaivre, west of Hawkesbury, Ontario, needed all the syrup they could get to serve up a record-breaking pancake. Local Lions Club members mixed, poured, flipped and cooked a 9.14-metre-wide flapjack that weighed 909 kilograms.

 # Mortal Danger

In early April, 1996, keepers of Wiarton Willie announced that the famed weather-predicting gopher from Wiarton, Ontario, was being kept in protective custody. Town officials were responding to death threats made by angry callers who felt Willie had let them down. He had promised everyone an early spring, but winter was still hanging around.

Three years later, a long line of mourners paid their last respects to the shadow-fearing critter. News of Wiarton Willie's death from natural causes brought messages of condolence from around the world. But sympathy turned to anger once again when people who had filed past the tiny wooden casket learned that the stiff little body in the coffin was a pretender to the weather-predicting throne.

When keepers had gone to check on Willie in his den and make sure he was ready to make an appearance on February 2, Groundhog Day, they were shocked to find that he had passed away sometime during the winter . . . and what was left of him wasn't a pretty sight. So they tucked a stuffed, glass-eyed substitute into the coffin and displayed it to the thousands of visitors attending the Wiarton Willie Winter Festival. Saddened mourners said they felt betrayed. *Really?*

Smelling a Rat

Some Halifax residents got a bit of a scare on February 2, 2000, during radio station CFRQ's coverage of a local version of Wiarton Willie's weather-predicting efforts. Claiming that the city wouldn't spend money for a real groundhog, the station reported that a sewer rat — Waterfront Willie — had been recruited instead.

But when the time came for the waterfront rat to make his debut, a news announcer reporting live by cellphone said Willie wouldn't come out and he was going to poke him with a stick. Then the horrified-sounding reporter started describing in gory detail how the enraged Willie was tearing into the limbs of city officials on hand for the ceremonies. Suddenly the cellphone went dead . . . and the station's switchboard lit up. Worried listeners wanted to know what had happened to the announcer. That's when the real announcers decided to come clean. There was no Waterfront Willie, and the report of carnage was a fake. The whole thing had just been a hoax intended to spice up a bland February morning.

DID YOU KNOW...

. . . that there are no skunks in Newfoundland? And Alberta does an excellent job of keeping out rats. Although a few have been known to slip in uninvited, officially there are no rats in the province.

Pass the Pickles

Some people will do almost anything to set a new world record. In 1978, Patrick Donahue made a grab for his fifteen minutes of fame in Victoria, B.C. That's where he wolfed down 91 pickled onions in just 1 minute and 8 seconds. The price of glory? Onion burps and a bloated belly.

Thank goodness no official was around to enforce a law that's supposedly still included in Canada's criminal code. Apparently, it's illegal to offend a public place with a bad smell.

Long, Longer, Longest

If you're into making long trips, Canada is definitely the place to be. The ultimate challenge would be to hike along or sail in and out of every bay and inlet along Canada's coastline, the longest in the world. As Statistics Canada points out, if it were stretched out into a straight line, it would reach two-thirds of the way to the moon.

A somewhat saner trip would be a drive across the country on the world's longest national highway, the Trans-Canada Highway. It's 7821 kilometres long. If you prefer a shorter journey that's still pretty impressive, you can wend your way from Toronto to Rainy River, Ontario, on the longest street in the world. Yonge Street, Toronto's main thoroughfare, reaches all the way to the Ontario-Minnesota border, a distance of more than 1900 kilometres.

And if you just want to spend a few hours breathing in brisk winter air, you can head to Ottawa and glide along the world's longest skating rink, a 7.8-kilometre section of the Rideau Canal. Daily traffic and weather reports even include updated information on ice conditions for those hardy commuters who skate to work each morning.

Bridging the Gap

Confederation Bridge links New Brunswick to Prince Edward Island. There's no question about it — at 12.9 kilometres, this engineering wonder is the longest bridge in the world built over water that's sometimes ice-covered. But another question remains: is an island still an island if you can get there by car? That's under debate in P.E.I., the province that's been dubbed the biggest farm in Canada. (By the way, the dirt there really is red.)

Kissing Bridge

The 339-metre-long wooden bridge at Hartland, New Brunswick, is one of Canada's most popular tourist attractions. It's the longest covered bridge in the world. Some people think that the bridge was covered over to keep out the snow, but that's not true. Locals actually used to haul snow onto the bridge so that horse-drawn sleighs could cross it easily in the winter. But covers on bridges like this one did keep them drier and stop the wooden planks from rotting too quickly. They also kept spying neighbours from watching courting couples as they drove across the bridge in carriages or sleighs. That's why they were often called kissing bridges.

The Ice Man Rules

Jimmy "The Ice Man" MacNeil rode his Zamboni with pride. Fans at the Brantford, Ontario, Civic Centre cheered him on whenever he drove his big ice scraper out between periods of Junior B hockey games. But he got a lot more than local recognition when an email contest to choose the best Zamboni driver in North America caught fire during the summer and fall of 1999. When Brantford fans learned of the contest, they nominated their very own Ice Man, and then began to spread the word. MacNeil was definitely the underdog, going up against Zamboni drivers from some of the National Hockey League's top arenas. But Canadians — some of the world's heaviest users of the Internet — rallied around him, and their votes started flooding in. To the amazement of contest organizers, MacNeil won the contest. He was the new North American Zamboni champion!

NHL officials hadn't expected this result. The winner was slated to clean the ice during the All-Star game on February 6, 2000, at the Toronto Maple Leaf's new home, the Air Canada Centre. But the regular Air Canada Centre Zamboni drivers weren't about to let the supposedly inexperienced MacNeil loose on their ice. Still, MacNeil wasn't bitter. He did get to drive a ceremonial victory lap around the arena.

How Low Can You Go?

Probably not as low as 15-year-old Marlene Raymond did when she limboed under a flaming bar at the Port of Spain Pavilion during Toronto's Caravan Festival in 1973. On June 24 that year she set a new world record for limbo dancing when she cleared a burning bar that was just 16.5 centimetres off the ground!

Big Apples

Canada's own McIntosh apple is a really big hit around the world. It's so well recognized as something wonderfully delicious that it's even used as the logo for a top-brand computer. Over half of the 17 million or so bushels of apples grown in Canada every year are crisp, juicy Macs, and every one of them can be traced back to one tree that farmer John McIntosh found growing on his St. Lawrence River Valley farm in 1811.

No one knows for certain how that apple tree came to be growing in the woods McIntosh was clearing at his new homestead. But we do know that if his son, Allan, hadn't figured out how to graft cuttings from it onto other apple trees, there wouldn't be any McIntosh apples around today.

Another Canadian big apple catches the eye of every traveller on Ontario's Highway 401 near Colborne, Ontario. You can't miss it. It's bright red — naturally — and it's 10.7 metres tall and 11.6 metres wide. This 42-tonne structure doubles as a restaurant and tourist information site in a region of the country very proud of the apples grown there. Ontario produces about 400 million Macs a year.

Top Dog

On October 5, 1990, children's author Jean Little received an honourary doctorate from Ontario's University of Guelph, in her own home town.

Little was named a "doctor of letters, *honoris causa*." But she wasn't the only one in the spotlight at that graduation ceremony. University president Brian Segal presented Little's seeing-eye dog, Zephyr, with his own special degree: "doctor of litters, *honoris canine*." Little accepted the honour on Zephyr's behalf. Having guided his owner safely to the stage, the Labrador retriever was settled down beside her, snoozing.

The Labrador retriever is a Canadian breed of dog. Both black and golden Labs often graduate with top honours from schools that train dogs to guide the blind. One of the breed also achieved hero status on December 11, 1919.

On that fateful day, the SS *Ethie*, battered by hurricane-force winds, ran aground off the west coast of Newfoundland, north of the Bay of Islands. One sailor shot a rope from the boat to the shore, but it fell short among some offshore rocks. Local residents couldn't reach it, but one of their dogs did. The brave animal fought its way through the huge icy waves breaking over the rocks, bit onto the end of the line, and swam with it back to shore. With the rope secured, all 60 passengers and 32 crew members aboard the *Ethie* were eventually rescued.

An Owner's Manual for a Hat?

That's right. There is a hat that actually comes with a four-page owner's manual, and it's very, very Canadian. The manual for the made-in-Canada Tilley Hat tells you how to wear it, how to clean it, and — in case you can't figure it out on your own — how to tell the front from the back. It even tells you how to rescue the hat if it falls overboard when you're sailing.

The creation of Torontonian Alex Tilley in 1980, this hat has become the darling of travellers around the world. Canadian peacekeepers wear it proudly abroad, and it was Everest-climber Sir Edmund Hillary's favourite headgear. One reason for the Tilley hat's popularity is that it's nearly indestructible. And if it does wear out, you can get a replacement for free. But that's not likely to be necessary. One Tilley owner claims that an elephant ate his hat, and when the hat "re-emerged" a day later, a good wash was all it needed. Good thing — the elephant ate the hat not just once, but three times!

Another Top Hat

Another made-in-Canada hat that took the world by storm was the jaunty red Roots creation Canadian athletes wore at the 1998 Winter Olympics in Nagano, Japan. It was such a hot item that the athletes had a hard time keeping it on their heads. The "poor boy" caps quickly became a hit with celebrities looking to make a fashion statement, too. Without an owner's manual to guide them, some people wore it backwards, but that didn't matter. It looked great either way.

These Shoes Aren't Meant for Walking

The world's biggest and best collection of shoes, boots, sandals and everything else related to footwear is housed in the Bata Shoe Museum in Toronto. The museum's 10 000-piece collection covers 4500 years of footwear history. It's also home to such cool items as Elvis Presley's blue-and-white patent leather loafers, prima ballerina Karen Kain's pointe shoes, Elton John's silver platform boots, Queen Victoria's satin flats and the Nike trainers David Bowie wore on his Serious Moonlight tour.

What's That, Eh?

Want to nosh on a Pogo? Pogo is the brand name for a Canadian-made junk food treat. Popular first in Quebec, it's now even available in the frozen food section of the supermarket. Haven't had one yet? Well, it's a hot dog dipped in cornmeal batter that's then deep-fried or baked, and served on a stick.

Ketchup or Vinegar?

Canada is the world's largest producer of frozen french fries. Maritime food giant McCain Foods Ltd. can take credit for this Canadian claim to fame.

And just for the record, instant mashed potatoes are a Canadian invention. They were first cooked up by Edward Asselbergs, a research scientist with Canada's Department of Agriculture. He patented his flaky recipe in 1961.

On the west coast, Pemberton, British Columbia, can claim its share of spud glory. Although a sign at the outskirts of town warns, "The planting of potatoes is prohibited," Pemberton is home to nearly 170 fields of potatoes. But these aren't just any old potatoes. Pemberton spuds are started in sterile labs and planted in carefully tended fields to make sure that they are free of diseases that commonly attack potato plants. That's why they are in such demand as seed potatoes with many North American growers. It's also why any unauthorized growing of potatoes is strictly forbidden.

Summer Never Came

People in Canada and the northern United States liked to keep a copy of *The Old Farmer's Almanac* handy. Published annually, this small book contains all sorts of interesting news, household hints and farming advice. It also offers weather predictions for the entire next year. In 1815, one of the typesetters preparing the 1816 almanac for printing decided to have a little fun. He slipped in a fake prediction of snow, hail and rain for July 13, 1816. Imagine everyone's surprise months later when it did exactly that.

And not just on that day. On June 5, bitter Arctic winds had swept through eastern Canada, killing crops in the fields and leaves on the trees, and giving people in Quebec and Montreal a major snowstorm. And if that wasn't enough, the area was hit with a killer frost at the beginning of August, and another major snowfall on August 21.

Not surprisingly, 1816 became known as the "year without a summer." It was also the year when many people who had ended up with one of those altered copies of the almanac became faithful followers of the almanac's year-in-advance weather forecasts.

Just a Kid

In 2000, famed hockey great Henri "The Pocket Rocket" Richard was still younger than all the National Hockey League players who joined the NHL forty years after he did. How? Well, if you're counting birthdays, he just turned 16 in 2000. That's because his birthday is February 29, and that day usually only comes around once every four years. The former Montreal Canadiens star is one of about 21 000 Canadians who are leap-year babies. In non-leap years, most of them choose to celebrate their big day on February 28. They might have had to do that again in 2000 if that number couldn't be divided evenly by 400. Unless a turn-of-the-century year — such as 1800, 1900, 2000 or 2100 — is divisible by 400, leaving no remainder, it isn't a leap year. Then "leapers" have to wait *another* four years for their official big day.

DID YOU KNOW...

... that the Stanley Cup, awarded each year to the champions of the National Hockey League, is one of the very few major professional sports trophies that players can take home and show off to their friends? And did you know that Kenora, Ontario, is the smallest community ever to give the cup a home for a year? It happened when the Kenora Thistles won the championship in 1907.

Hoop Dreams

Next to soccer, basketball is the most popular sport in the world, and all those exciting slam dunks can be traced right back to James Naismith, the Canadian from Almonte, Ontario, who invented the game. Naismith came up with the idea of trying to shoot a soccer ball through a peach basket on December 21, 1891, when he was working as a physical education director at a YMCA in Springfield, Massachusetts. Over the next few weeks, Naismith tidied up his rules for the new indoor sport, and the first proper game was played in January, 1892.

Fifty-four years later, Canadians again made basketball history. On November 1, 1946, the Toronto Huskies hosted the New York Knicks at Toronto's Maple Leaf Gardens. This match was, in effect, the first National Basketball League game ever played. The Huskies were one of the founding members of the Basketball Association of America, which went on to become the NBA. However, the Huskies only lasted a year. They also lost that first game against the Knicks 68–66.

Silent Terror

On March 30, 1848, people living near Niagara Falls woke up to a terrifying sound — the sound of silence. The night before, so much ice had built up in Lake Erie that it had dammed up the water that usually poured into the Niagara River and raced over the Falls. But local residents didn't know this. All they knew was that the never-ending torrent that had become so familiar to them was gone. When they dressed and rushed to the river's edge, they stood in awe. The Falls had stopped falling!

Some people were so worried by this unnatural sight that they rushed off to attend special church services held to calm their fears. A few more daring folks took advantage of this once-in-a-lifetime chance to scramble over the rocks at the bottom of the Falls, or to walk across the mighty river that had been reduced to a trickle.

The next night, changing winds broke up the ice-jam and water started to surge out of the lake and into the river once more. In just a matter of minutes, water from the Falls was falling again. The familiar roar was music to people's ears.

FALLS STOPS FALLING!

Unbelievable!

On July 9, 1960, seven-year-old Roger Woodward and his seventeen-year-old sister, Deanne, went for a Saturday afternoon boat ride with a family friend, Jim Honeycutt. After several minutes putt-putting down the Niagara River, the boat's propeller hit a rock and broke. Without power, the boat was caught in the grip of the river's surging current. Honeycutt started rowing furiously, but the boat capsized in the rushing water, tossing the terrified threesome overboard.

Roger and Deanne were both wearing life jackets, but they were no match for the river. Just a few metres from the Falls, Deanne was grabbed by a quick-thinking bystander, but Roger and Honeycutt were swept over the brink. Incredibly, as Roger tumbled into the swirling whirlpool below, he was spotted by the captain of the *Maid of the Mist*, a boat that regularly takes tourists on the ride of their lives beneath the Falls. Young Roger managed to grab hold of a life preserver thrown from the boat. When he was hauled to safety on board, the first thing he asked for, trembling and gasping, was a drink of water.

Both Roger and his sister recovered completely from their brush with death, but the Falls had claimed one more victim. Honeycutt's body was found four days later.

Out in
Left Field?

The year 1999 was a great year for CPRC — Circles
Phenomenon Research Canada. It's a group that tracks
and studies the sudden mysterious appearances of
circular shapes in farmers' fields. In 1999 the group
recorded a record number of crop circles in Canada, 20
in all. Saskatchewan, a popular gallery for such geometric
field art, topped the list with 10. The circles showed up
in prairie wheat fields, blueberry fields and cornfields in
six provinces.

Many people think the shapes are the work of pranksters
who sneak into the fields at night and trample down the
plants. Others say unusual swirling winds cause them. But
CPRC members aren't so sure what's going on. Still, they
aren't ready to blame aliens either — the usual suspects
when easy explanations are hard to come by.

Firefighters got more than they bargained for when they answered an alarm in a Montreal apartment building early in February, 2000. When they broke into a smoke-filled flat, they didn't have too much trouble putting out the fire. But they weren't too sure how to handle the big boa constrictor and 1.5-metre-long alligator left to guard the hundreds of marijuana plants growing in the place. The plants' owners were nowhere to be found.

That same month, a Winnipeg teenager was very happy to be found when firefighters arrived at her home. In fact, Rhiannon Bruyère says she might have died of smoke inhalation if it hadn't been for her animal housemate. She woke up in the middle of the night to find her tiny black kitten, Daisy, pawing at her face. Then she smelled the smoke. Thanks to Daisy, Bruyère and two other residents were able to escape to safety.

. . . that moose were once used to haul mail in the Edmonton area? Caribou also did the job in Labrador every now and then.

DID YOU KNOW...

. . . that the first recorded baseball game played in North America took place in Beachville, Ontario, on June 4, 1838, one year before Abner Doubleday's supposed "invention" of the game in Cooperstown, New York?

 # Maple Hits a Home Run

For nearly 70 years, batters in major league baseball games could use only bats made from ash trees. But when the new season opened in the spring of 1998, that rule changed. The league officially approved the use of the new Sam Bat, made by Ottawa carpenter Sam Holman. Holman makes his bats out of Canadian maple trees because maple is harder and doesn't dent or break as easily as ash. When the Baseball Hall of Fame in Cooperstown, New York, learned the Sam Bat had been approved, it got one to include in its hall of famous bats that have been swung into baseball history.

Larry Walker's bat was pretty special too. It took him all the way from his hometown of Maple Ridge, B. C., to the big leagues of professional baseball. Only a few Canadians have done that, and he was the first one of them to make it to the top. On November 13, 1997, the 30-year-old outfielder for the Colorado Rockies was named the most valuable player in the National League. Nine years later, Justin Morneau, another Canadian — and another British Columbian — matched Walker's achievement when he was named the American League's MVP for 2006.

Psssst . . .
Wanna Buy a Cup o' Poop?

If you did, then the tiny village of Desmond, Ontario, a few kilometres north of Napanee, was the place to go. Throughout most of the 1990s it claimed to be the manure capital of Ontario, and maybe of the world. For nine years it hosted "Manurefest," a celebration of you-know-what, and there was plenty of it to go around. You name it; they had it — from chickens, rabbits, sheep, pigs, horses and cows. If you were a serious gardener, you could pick up a 20-kilogram sack of the stuff. But if you just wanted to give one of your houseplants a boost, you could buy a "Cup o' Poop," a small bag of it neatly stuffed into a disposable coffee cup.

Better Late Than Never

In 1984, hockey superstar Wayne Gretzky was named to the Order of Canada. But winter's a busy time for someone with a job like Gretzky's, and he was doing his rather well, so he couldn't make it to the ceremonies in Ottawa to receive his medal. His team needed him then, and for the next 13 winters when the Order of Canada ceremonies were held.

But by January, 1998, Gretzky was playing for the New York Rangers, and they just happened to be in the capital to play the Ottawa Senators. Finally the Great One was able to visit Rideau Hall when the Order of Canada ceremonies were taking place. So, on January 28, 1998 — 14 years later — Gretzky proudly received his medal from Governor General Roméo LeBlanc.

The **Great** One Is the Greatest

During his career, Gretzky tied or broke an incredible 61 records — some of them his own. Here's just a sampling of his record-breaking accomplishments:
• most regular season career goals (894 in 1487 games)
• most goals, including playoff games (1016)
• most goals in one season (92)
• most regular season career assists (1962)
• most assists, including playoffs (2222)
• most career points, including playoffs (3238)
• most 100-or-more point seasons (15)
• most career playoff goals (122)
• most career playoff assists (260)
• most game-winning playoff goals (24)

In 1999, Gretzky bid farewell to the sport he loved with a passion, and the National Hockey League retired his jersey number, 99, forever.

If You Can't Beat Them, Join Them

Janet and Gerry McKay called their farm at Rimbey, north of Red Deer, Alberta, the Bloomin' Idiot Funny Farm. Like the rest of us, the McKays had to put up with buzzing, blood-hungry mosquitoes during the summer months. But instead of crying in their insect repellent, they finally decided to befriend the enemy. They set up little houses where "mozzies" could breed in peace, and in 1994, they founded SWAMP, the Society for Wild Alberta Mosquito Preservation. Then they started selling lifetime memberships in SWAMP to other "Bloomin' Idiots." Members got tiny playground toys and a miniature outhouse to make mosquitoes feel right at home.

In 1998, the McKays started pushing for a special national Mosquito Appreciation Day — MAD. They figured January 31 would be a great choice for MAD, since on that day you'd have to hold off swatting any of the annoying little pests. The idea didn't catch on.

Researchers in Winnipeg say that Canadian mosquitoes are nastier than most of the other 3000 or so species found throughout the world. You'll get no argument about that from people in Manitoba. Supposedly, it ties with Louisiana as the mosquito capital of North America.

Doing the Salt Crawl

If you decided to take a dip in Patience Lake, southeast of Saskatoon, Saskatchewan, you wouldn't have to worry too much about sinking. The water in Patience Lake is ten times saltier than sea water, making it denser and much easier to float in than fresh water. But Patience Lake isn't as unusual as you might think. More than 500 Saskatchewan lakes, ranging in size from 4 to 180 square metres, are salty.

What's That, Eh?

According to *The Canadian Oxford Dictionary, keener* is a Canadian term used to describe the type of student most teachers wished they had more of in their classes. Neat, eh?

DID YOU KNOW...

...that, on average, the coldest day of the year in Canada is February 6? And the warmest? That's usually on or about July 17.

Muscle Power

Pedal power ruled in the spring of 1982 when Brock Allison set off from Vancouver on May 1, on a trip across Canada. On June 26 he arrived in Halifax. It had taken him 56 days and 10.75 hours to ride 5947.7 kilometres — on his unicycle!

Three years later, from August 10–12, 25-year-old David Frank rode his skateboard back and forth and around and around in Toronto. He pushed and rolled 432.77 kilometres in 36 hours, 43 minutes, 42 seconds — earning himself a place in the record books.

And two years after that, in February, 1987, John Sarish showed off his record-breaking muscle power in London, Ontario, by pushing a wheelbarrow 74.07 metres. So what's the big deal? Well, the wheelbarrow was loaded with 3781.36 kilograms of bricks.

Frequent Flyers

During the summer months, brightly coloured orange, black and white monarch butterflies are always on the move, flitting from flower to flower to fuel up on nectar. But when the days start to get shorter and the nights a little cooler, they set out on an incredible 4000-kilometre journey all the way from southern Canada to central Mexico. Many of them don't make it, but about 300 million do. The spring migration north is a more leisurely affair. It takes three or four generations of monarchs to complete the trip back to Canada. How does each new butterfly know where to go when it emerges from its chrysalis? That is still a mystery.

How Bad Was It?

The Great Depression of the 1930s was a very difficult time for many Canadians. Hundreds of thousands were out of work, and hungry people were forced to line up at government- or charity-run soup kitchens for free meals. Farmers on the drought-stricken prairies went broke, and city families who couldn't pay the rent lost their homes. But even hard times can produce some pretty tricky folk sayings. One popular Canadian saying that referred to someone wearily trudging from place to place looking for a job said it all: "His shoes were so thin, he could step on a dime and tell whether it was heads or tails."

And if you were wondering just how flat the prairie landscape could be, some Manitobans might point out that it's so flat and bare that "a woodpecker would have to pack a box lunch."

Speaking of Canadian folk sayings, here's one that a grandmother could use when a visiting grandchild was behaving so unbelievably well that she wondered what was up. She'd look the little angel in the eye and say, "You're so sweet, you make my teeth ache."

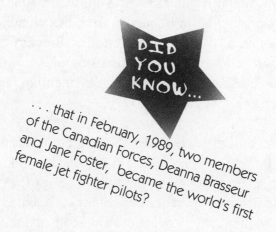

DID YOU KNOW...

. . . that in February, 1989, two members of the Canadian Forces, Deanna Brasseur and Jane Foster, became the world's first female jet fighter pilots?

Snowballs

April 7, 1977 . . . Spring training had ended and the baseball season was underway. Over 44 500 eager fans crowded into Toronto's Exhibition Stadium for the very first home game of the Toronto Blue Jays. But by the end of the game it wasn't just the new Canadian team's uniforms that were blue. The *fans* were turning blue too. It snowed during the game and, with the wind chill factored in, it was –10°C in the outdoor stadium. Thank goodness the Jays pulled off a 9–5 win over the Chicago White Sox. At least the fans went home with warm hearts.

Tree Tops

Of the ten biggest trees in North America, six are found in beautiful British Columbia, and they're all Western red cedars. Biggest doesn't mean tallest. It's a combination of height, trunk thickness and how wide the branching, leafy top (crown) spreads out.

The tallest tree in Canada is a Sitka spruce in B.C.'s Carmanah Pacific Provincial Park. This majestic spruce towers nearly 96 metres above the ground. Another B.C. giant, a Douglas fir in Strathcona Provincial Park, comes second at just under 83 metres.

What's That, Eh?

Don't expect visitors to know what you're talking about the first time you mention a loony (also loonie) or a toony (also toonie or twoonie). You may be too young to remember what life was like before these two coins replaced the one- and two-dollar bills, so you might not realize that these terms are just nicknames, and not official terms for the currency.

Hold Your Tongue, or Else . . .

. . . You'll lose it. At one time that was the warning given to residents of New France. The eighth time you were caught using profanity could be your last. The punishment for an eighth violation of the no-dirty-language order was very effective — cut out the offending tongue.

Get Me Outta Here!

One big problem early Canada had to cope with was fire. Entire settlements could be reduced to charred rubble by fires that started in dirty soot-filled chimneys, so regular chimney cleaning was often compulsory. However, people obviously didn't pay too much attention to the poor chimney sweeps who had to crawl down into the chimneys and clean them out. Why else would the *Quebec Gazette* have printed a notice to readers in September, 1772, reminding them to put out fires in the fireplaces before the sweeps started work?

What's That, Eh?

Ski-doo isn't just a brand name anymore. The original name given by Armand Bombardier to his invention has now become a Canadian word in and of itself. Companies other than Bombardier must become a little frustrated when people call their products skidoos and talk about going skidooing.

Great Lakes

The Great Lakes really are great. Superior, with surface area of 82 414 square kilometres, is the largest freshwater lake in the world. What's more, Canada has nine of the ten largest freshwater lakes in North America. Starting with the largest, they are: Lake Superior (obviously), Lake Huron, Great Bear Lake, Great Slave Lake, Lake Erie, Lake Winnipeg, Lake Ontario, Lake Athabaska, and Reindeer Lake. Lake Michigan, in the U.S., comes in at third largest in North America, right after Lake Huron.

And in the middle of one of those great lakes lies the largest fresh-water island in the world — Manitoulin Island in Lake Huron. Manitoulin is big enough to have its own island in a lake. So, that island — Mindemoya — is an island in a lake on an island in a lake. Got that?

DID YOU KNOW...

. . . that most Christmas trees sold during the holiday season are 10 years old when they're cut down?

That's Some Log Cabin

Montebello, Quebec, west of Montreal, is home to Le Château Montebello. This impressive resort hotel has the distinction of being the biggest log building in the world. Erected in 1930 by the Canadian Pacific Railway (CPR), it was built out of 100 000 red cedar logs brought by train all the way from British Columbia. More than 3000 men, working mainly by hand, assembled the logs in just two months, a feat nearly as impressive as the building itself.

DID YOU KNOW...

. . . that the popular, easy-to-use square-headed screw and matching square-ended screwdriver are Canadian inventions? Peter L. Robertson of Milton, Ontario, invented them in 1908, and to this day the screwdriver bears his name.

It's A Bird ... It's A Plane ... It's A Star!

It may seem hard to believe, but far too many Canadians have never really seen the night sky. Because of all the light pollution in areas where most Canadians live, the night sky appears as a pale imitation of the real thing. Even on the clearest of nights the glow of big cities still outshines the spectacular beauty of the heavens.

But in 1997 Ontario became the first place in the world with a dark-sky park. A 1900-hectare piece of province-owned land known as the Torrance Barrens is preserved as a light-free zone. Like provincial and national parks set aside to protect plant and animal life and the natural landscape, the area south of Lake Muskoka and west of Gravenhurst protects the skyscape from light pollution. All together now: "Twinkle, twinkle, little star . . . "

Silence is Golden

It used to be illegal in Manitoba to sing while using "the facilities," if the outhouse was attached to an eating establishment or tavern where wine was served. Who knows what riotous melodies might have drifted through the walls into the dining room if that law hadn't been in place. As for what else might have drifted through the walls, that's another story . . .

51

Liar, Liar

Elected members still have to watch what they say when they're debating in Parliament and provincial legislatures. None of them can call another member a liar — it's an example of "unparliamentary language." The forbidden word list for Members of Parliament also includes such choice phrases as "bag of wind," "evil genius" and "political sewer pipes." In the Ontario legislature, "vulture" is taboo, and "fat, wingless duck" is a no-no in Alberta.

DID YOU KNOW...

. . . that the Peace Tower in the centre block of the Parliament buildings in Ottawa is among the largest monuments to peace in the world?

Towering Above the Rest

When it was built in 1975, Toronto's amazing 555-metre-high CN Tower was the tallest free-standing structure in the world. (It has now been surpassed by the Burj Dubai.) On a clear day, when you look out from the observation floor at the 447-metre level, you can see all the way across Lake Ontario to Niagara Falls.

George Kapeynes of Hamilton, Ontario, didn't show up at the Tower on October 27, 1985, to do some sightseeing, though. He was there to climb its 1760 stairs, and he did it in a record-breaking 8 minutes, 28 seconds.

. . . that at the turn of the millennium, Canadians were drinking about 15 billion cups of coffee and about 7 billion cups of tea a year? But nearly 5 million Canucks probably switch to things like hot lemon juice and honey or chicken soup for a week or two each winter. Why? Because up to 5 million Canadians get the flu annually.

Not Very Ladylike, Eh?

On May 30, 1899, a Canadian woman named Pearl Hart pulled off the last stagecoach hold-up in the United States. After finishing her regular education, Hart had gone to a special finishing school for proper young ladies in her home town of Lindsay, Ontario. But then she ran away from home and ended up in Colorado, where she hung out with Martha Jane Canary — better known as Calamity Jane — a sharp-shooting star of Wild West shows, and the girlfriend of Wild Bill Hickok.

Bird on the Run

On November 6, 1997, a fugitive named Elisha was spotted on the Ottawa River trying to hide out among a flock of Canada geese. But she stood out like a pink flamingo in that crowd, and it wasn't long before some worried bird-watchers were hot on her trail.

Elisha was in fact a real flamingo that had escaped back in early September from a greenhouse on her wealthy owner's New England estate. After a month of outwitting her American pursuers, she went into hiding. Now she was back in plain view, but no one could catch her, and time was running out. With winter on the way, Elisha was in danger of starving or freezing to death. Finally, in mid-December, some volunteers managed to snag her in the river with a net. So, Ottawans said goodbye to Elisha and to any fantasies they might have had about living in the new Florida of the north.

Linked to the Past

It all started on March 11, 1965. That's the day Gary Duschl of Waterdown, near Hamilton, Ontario, first picked up a Wrigley's gum wrapper, tore it in half lengthwise, and after a few careful folds, slipped one part into the other to form the first two links of a gum wrapper chain. Kids have been making gum wrapper chains ever since Wrigley's first came out with Juicy Fruit, Spearmint and Doublemint, so what Duschl did that day wasn't a big deal. But the fact that he's still adding to that chain decades later is.

By 2000 Duschl's chain was more than 8 kilometres long and weighed about 170 kilograms. Lying in bins in his basement, it looked like a long, thin yellow-and-green snake waiting to slither out onto the floor. Ripley's Entertainment offered to buy it for one of its Believe It or Not! museums, but Duschl said no. He had only linked up about 650 000 wrappers by then, and he was aiming for a million.

By the mid-2000s Duschl folded his way well past the million-gum wrapper mark, and by March 2009, he had linked 1 370 166 wrappers together to make a chain 17 760 metres long.

THE Gardens

It's been dubbed the "temple of hockey." It's also been called "Make-Believe Gardens" because of how loyal Toronto Maple Leaf fans remain even though their team hasn't won a Stanley Cup championship since 1967. Built in 1931, the Gardens quickly became the best known hockey arena in all of North America. It was home to the Leafs until they moved to the new Air Canada Centre in February, 1999.

But hockey isn't the Gardens' only claim to fame. British prime minister Winston Churchill gave a speech in the Gardens over 70 years ago. Elvis Presley drove the girls wild at two back-to-back Gardens concerts in 1957, and the Beatles had fans fainting all over the place when they played there in 1964. And in 1966, Canadian boxer George Chuvalo went face to face with the heavyweight champion of the world, Muhammad Ali. That match made boxing history. Ali won the fight, but Chuvalo was the only opponent ever to last a full 15 rounds with the king of the ring.

And speaking of Elvis . . .

Elvis Presley went on to Ottawa following his Gardens appearance in April, 1957. There he gave two more performances that definitely left those in attendance all shook up. The next day, April 4, a local newspaper reported that eight young ladies had been expelled from Notre Dame Convent for disobeying a school ban against attending such an immoral event.

Elvis never got to give his next scheduled concert in Verdun, Quebec. That event was cancelled to prevent the corruption of local youth. Four months later, on August 31, Elvis returned to Canada to perform in front of a crowd of 25 000 at Empire Stadium in Vancouver. The show ended after just 45 minutes when rioting fans rushed onto the field.

Those three "Elvis sightings" put Canada on the trivia map as the only foreign country The King ever performed in.

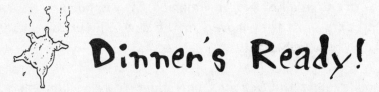 # Dinner's Ready!

Cooks in Elgin, Manitoba, had an easy time of it on April 22, 1932. The main course landed in town, cooked and ready to serve, when lightning bolts struck a flock of wild geese flying overhead. The zapped birds fell to the ground crisp and sizzling, so there was no point in letting them go to waste.

All Bugged Up

Early computers were giants when compared to today's desktops and laptops, but they weren't nearly as "smart" as the newer mini-models. In fact, one computer was an absolute dunce. In 1965 the Ministry of Education in Quebec put one of the new-fangled machines to work marking province-wide Grade 11 exams. It failed miserably, making mistakes correcting every single one of the 7000 tests. Give that computer an F!

Winnie the Canuck

The English claim him as their own. He's Christopher Robin's lovable bear buddy, Winnie-the-Pooh. Created by an English writer, A. A. Milne, the character was based on a small black bear named Winnie who was a hugely popular resident of the London Zoo. But residents of White River, Ontario, northwest of Sault Ste. Marie, know better. They know that the original Winnie is Canadian through and through.

In 1913, a trapper found an orphaned black bear cub and took her to White River where she could be fed and cared for. A year later a Canadian veterinarian, Harry Colebourn, spotted the bear when the train taking him to Toronto to join other World War I soldiers stopped in White River. Colebourn bought the bear, named her Winnie after his home town, Winnipeg, and took her with him to England as the mascot of his army regiment, the 2nd Canadian Infantry Brigade. Winnie was sent to the London Zoo when the regiment left to fight in France. Milne and his son, Christopher Robin, were two of the many visitors who loved to go to the zoo to watch Winnie.

And that's how a Canadian bear got a starring role in a British children's classic, and why both White River and Winnipeg have statues honouring the world-famous, honey-loving resident of Pooh Corner.

Christmas Crush

Robert Waller worked as a clerk at the Wal-Mart store in Fredericton, New Brunswick. On December 14, 1996, he was injured on the job. He was rushed to hospital with a concussion, several broken ribs, an injured back and leg, and cuts and bruises over much of his body. He was off work for six months recovering from those injuries.

Did the store roof or a huge stack of cast-iron pots come crashing down on Waller? No. What hit him was a crowd of frenzied Christmas shoppers. They trampled him underfoot when they spotted him opening a box of newly arrived Tickle Me Elmo dolls. The dolls were all the rage that year, and some people were willing to pay thousands of dollars to get one. Waller was just one of many unfortunate victims struck down by the Elmo virus. Bah, humbug.

Mega-Sizzlers

When the J. M. Schneider Company and M&M Meats in Kitchener, Ontario, got together on a sausage-making feat, they were unbeatable. In September, 1983, they stuffed a 14.17-kilometre-long sausage coil with nearly 7950 kilograms of ground pork and seasonings. In 1990, a team in England knocked them off the Guinness record podium with a 21-kilometre-long effort. But in 1997 the Kitchener team was back with a vengeance. Over two days in April, they ground out a 46-kilometre-long whopper.

All Shook Up in Cottage Country

The T-shirt reads: I SPENT THE WEEKEND WITH ELVIS IN COLLINGWOOD. But maybe it should actually read: I spent the weekend with *lots* of Elvises, because hundreds of them, complete with sequin-covered jumpsuits and slicked-back hair, turn up in Collingwood, Ontario, each summer for the annual Canadian Elvis Tribute and Convention. The first Collingwood Elvisfest was held July 28–30, 1995. Ever since that first success, thousands of visitors have crowded into Collingwood for a week or so to step on each other's blue suede shoes, and they can't help falling in love with the place. Little sisters, hard-headed women and bossa nova babies gather to cheer on their big hunks of love who are hoping to win prizes for the best sideburns, the best jumpsuit, and the best on-stage imitation. Judges know it may be now or never for some of the older E.P. wannabes, so they hand out a prize for the oldest Elvis, too.

Big Nickel

On a clear day, you can't miss it. It's the Big Nickel — Sudbury, Ontario's, best-known landmark — and it really is big. It's 9 metres across and 61 centimetres thick, making it the largest coin in the world. This giant replica of a 1951 five-cent piece marks the entrance to the Big Nickel Mine, the only hardrock mine in Ontario that is open to visitors. The mine gives tourists a glimpse into the life of a hardrock miner, and is also home to the only underground mailbox in Canada.

One item that uses up at least 25 000 tonnes of nickel a year is the stainless steel sink found in kitchens around the world. It was the brainchild of Harry Galley, who was born in Arundel, Quebec. Galley was an Inco sales executive. In the 1930s, he got the idea to replace enamel-coated cast-iron sinks with stainless

steel ones that wouldn't chip and were very easy to clean. But it wasn't until the 1940s that Inco agreed to pay for developing his idea in a serious way. Galley finally patented his sink design in 1948, and the rest is kitchen history.

Sanitation for the Nation

That was the motto of G. H. Wood and Co. Ltd., a company founded by George Hutchence Wood of Toronto, Ontario. Worried about the way diseases could spread when people shared the same drinking cup, especially in public places, he started a company to make paper-shaped cones. *Voilà* — the first disposable paper cup!

From 1950 to 1975, Wood's company display at the Canadian National Exhibition (CNE) wowed visitors to the annual fair. Each year Wood filled his display with a million dollars in bills, silver dollars and gold coins, to show everyone how much money businesses lost every day when people stayed home sick from illnesses caused by unhealthy, dirty workplaces. He prided himself in knowing that his company's sanitary products were in more public washrooms than any other firm's.

DID YOU KNOW... ... that Canada has two official sports? Lacrosse was most popular with Canadians until the 1900s and was the first organized sport in North America. Then hockey started to win over Canadian fans, and the debate was on as to which sport should have official status. Finally, in May, 1994, a bill giving both sports that honour became law.

Not Clever

One day in January, 1995, a would-be thief walked into a drugstore in Vernon, British Columbia, and told a clerk he was coming back in half an hour to rob the place. Sure enough, 30 minutes later he returned with a sidekick to help him carry out his big caper. But the two men barely made it in the door, let alone out of it with the loot. They walked right into the waiting arms of RCMP officers.

Double Duty

In 1858, John Butt was looking for work. He decided to go into business for himself in Victoria, British Columbia, a former fort that was quickly becoming a bustling new town. Butt offered his services to the town as a street cleaner, and worked out a fee to clean two streets — Governor Street and Yates Street — when they got really dirty. Then Butt set to work. First, he would scrape up and cart away the garbage, sludge and horse droppings from Governor Street. Then he'd drive to nearby Yates Street and, when no one was looking, he'd spread the filthy load there. After getting paid for cleaning Governor, he'd move along to Yates and get paid for cleaning *it*. And where did he put the filth from Yates? Right back on Governor! Victoria officials finally caught on to Butt's scam, but not before he had pocketed some decent change at the colony's expense.

In the Eye of the Beholder

Year after year, a giant steel magnet draws tourists to one of New Brunswick's most popular attractions, Magnetic Hill near Moncton. After driving up the famous hill, people put their cars in neutral and let them roll back down the hill. But as they roll down, their eyes tell them that they're actually rolling up the hill. It's all an optical illusion caused by the surrounding landscape — but knowing that doesn't spoil the fun. Visiting Magnetic Hill is just one of those things you have to do when you're on holiday.

Toilet Tales

Ever since 1977, Labour Day Weekend celebrations in Dawson City, Yukon, have included two special events — the Great International Outhouse Race and the Bathroom Wall Limerick Contest. The outhouse race is a 3-kilometre effort for four people in each five-member team that enters. They're the ones who actually carry their outhouse that far. The fifth member of the team has the privilege of sitting on the "throne" for the race through town. In the evening, teams gather at a local tavern to recite five-line limericks about their outhouse. Most of the verses are pretty . . . well . . . crappy.

Miraculous Recovery

No one is absolutely certain how little Karlee Kosolofski managed to slip out of her house in the wee hours of the morning on February 23, 1994. But the two-year-old from Regina, Saskatchewan, did exactly that on a bitterly cold night when temperatures plunged to -22°C. Karlee was outside in only her pyjamas for nearly six hours before she was found. By then her body temperature was just 14.2°C, way below the normal body temperature of about 37°C.

Karlee's parents thought she must be dead. Even doctors figured it was most unlikely that she could be revived. But they didn't give up hope. Over several hours they slowly and carefully warmed her little body and, amazingly, Karlee began to show signs of life.

Karlee did lose part of her left leg to frostbite, but her recovery was complete in every other way, and the "miracle child" became the first person in the world ever to survive such a low recorded body temperature.

DID YOU KNOW...

... that you can visit one of the best bonsai collections in the world right here in Canada? The marvellous miniature trees are growing in Montreal's Jardin Botanique.

Honouring a Japanese Tradition

You might not expect a Canadian stamp to have a picture of a sumo wrestler on it, but in June, 1998, Canada Post issued two such stamps. They celebrated a very special event that took place in Vancouver on June 6 and 7 that year. For only the ninth time in its 1500-year history, sumo wrestling held an official tournament, or *basho*, outside Japan. Vancouver's tournament was the first *basho* ever held in Canada.

Rulers of the Pumpkin Patch

Months of tender loving care finally paid off for pumpkin growers John and Chris Lyons on October 2, 1994. That day they presented their big baby for the official weigh-in at the annual Pumpkinfest held in Port Elgin, Ontario, and learned that it had set a new world record. It weighed in at an amazing 408 kilograms!

In 1999 two Canadians, Todd Kline and Al Eaton, stood second and third in a competition to grow the biggest Atlantic Giant Pumpkin, a breed favoured by growers serious about producing really, really big pumpkins. Kline's Giant weighed 471.13 kilograms and Eaton's was a 456.86-kilogram wonder. Now there's a jack-o'-lantern!

What's That, Eh?

If your cat chewed up part of your science fair project, and your little brother decorated the display board with his new markers, you might say that you're fed up with the whole shebang. No one's sure of the origin of *shebang*, but it popped up in Canada sometime in the nineteenth century, and it's still hanging around. "The whole shebang" means the whole situation, the whole lot or the whole thing.

Altona, Front and Centre

Want to find the geographic centre of North America? Then look no further than Altona, Manitoba, south of Winnipeg near the American border. But that's not the only reason to check out Altona. It's also known as the sunflower capital of Canada and, some say, maybe even of the world. To celebrate the famous local crop, Altona greets visitors with a pretty impressive roadside attraction — a giant painting that is 7.3 metres wide and 9.8 metres high, and mounted on a 24.4-metre-tall easel. And the picture on the easel? You guessed it — a still-life study of sunflowers!

What a Kid!

When 13-year-old Canadian diver Alexandre Despatie made his gold-medal platform dive at the 1998 Commonwealth Games in Kuala Lumpur, Malaysia, he entered the record books for more than his winning dive. He also became the world's youngest winner of an international diving competition.

A Generous Canadian

Canada's best known poem around the world is "In Flanders Fields." The poem was written by a Canadian army doctor, Lt.-Col. John McCrae, to remind people of the soldiers who gave their lives fighting in World War I. The poem, written in 1915, three years before McCrae died while serving in France, has touched the hearts of millions.

McCrae's war medals had been in the hands of a private collector for years, but were put up for sale in 1997. The trouble was, neither a museum dedicated to McCrae's memory nor the National War Museum in Ottawa could come up with the money — expected to top $20 000 — to buy them. Enter Toronto businessman Arthur Lee, who had come to Canada from China when he was 12.

People were concerned that the McCrae medals might be bought by someone who didn't live in Canada, and that this small but significant part of Canadian history would be lost to the country forever. Arthur Lee didn't know about their fears when he showed up at the auction, but about half an hour before the bidding began, he happened to read the poem and information about McCrae in a small brochure. The poem so moved Lee that, when the bidding on the medals soared to an amazing $300 000, he bid $400 000! The medals were his . . . but not for long. The next week, Lee donated them to what he felt was their rightful home — the McCrae Museum in Guelph, Ontario, John McCrae's home town.

. . . that Canada's most famous resident has his own postal code? To reach Mr. S. Claus at the North Pole, simply address your cards and letters to him at the Pole and add his code, H0H 0H0.

How long does it take him to reach all the good boys and girls each December? Supposedly, to finish his marathon sleigh ride in just 24 hours, he would have to travel at 112 kilometres per second, stopping for just 1/20 000th of a second at each chimney. Go, Santa!

They Did It First

Edward "Ned" Hanlan (1855–1908), a rower from Toronto, was Canada's first world champion athlete. Hanlan become the Canadian champion single sculler — that's a rower in a one-person lightweight boat — in 1877, and won the American championship in 1878. Then he headed off to England to take on the world champion, Australian E. A. Trickett, in 1879. Hanlan didn't just win. He beat Trickett to the

finish line by an amazing 11 lengths, and took home Canada's first world championship trophy.

In September, 1904, at the Olympic Games held in St. Louis, Missouri, Montrealer Étienne Desmarteau became the first Canadian to win Olympic gold for Canada. He came first in the 56-pound (25.45-kilogram) hammer throw event.

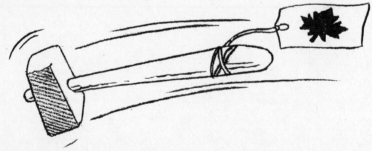

On September 20, 1954, Toronto long-distance swimmer Marilyn Bell became the first person ever to swim across Lake Ontario. She was just 16 at the time. A year later, she became the youngest person ever to swim across the English Channel.

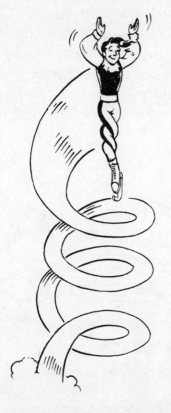

On March 25, 1988, Canadian figure skating champion Kurt Browning became the first person ever to complete a quadruple jump in competition. Doing the quad meant spinning around four times in the air before landing on one foot.

In the 1950s, Montreal Canadiens star Jacques Plante became the first goaltender to make a habit of skating around to the back of his net to stop the

puck and pass it to one of his teammates. And, fed up with getting hit in the face with a puck, he was also the first goalie to start wearing a mask regularly.

On September 23, 1992, Manon Rhéaume of Lac Beauport, Quebec, put on her mask and goalie pads and played one period of an NHL exhibition game for the Tampa Bay Lightning, making her the first woman ever to play NHL hockey.

In 1909, Toronto bowling alley operator Tom Ryan decided to make it easier for his customers to play the game. He made a smaller ball and replaced the ten heavy pins with five lighter ones, and so became the father of a brand new game — five-pin bowling.

DID YOU KNOW...

...that in both 2006 and 2007 a Canadian was chosen as the top American college female athlete of the year? Soccer all-star Christine Sinclair of Burnaby, British Columbia, won that award in 2006 while playing for the University of Portland, and Sarah Pavan of Kitchener, Ontario, won it in 2007 for her outstanding efforts on the University of Nebraska's championship volleyball team.

Phony as a Three-Dollar Bill?

Canadians used to have three-dollar bills, but they were officially done away with in 1871. Still, St. Stephen's Bank in New Brunswick kept on issuing them for another 15 years. And 25-cent bills weren't phony in Canada from 1870 to 1935. They were issued in 1870, 1900 and 1923, at times when there weren't enough quarters to go around. Because they weren't much bigger than a large Band-Aid, people called them "shinplasters." The Bank of Canada phased them out in 1935.

A Big Bonanza

You may have heard that Canada is home to the world's biggest *pysanka*, a brightly decorated Ukrainian Easter egg. Located in Vegreville, Alberta, it's 9.45 metres tall, 7.8 metres long and 5.5 metres wide.

And you've most likely heard of the Wawa Goose in Wawa, Ontario. This 2-tonne wrought-iron sculpture stands 9 metres tall, is 7 metres long, and is 6 metres wide from wingtip to wingtip.

But would you believe a 10.7-metre-long, 50-tonne lobster? Well, believe it. It's in Shediac, New Brunswick.

Naturally, Turtleford, Saskatchewan, has Big Ernie, an 8.5-metre-long turtle, and it seems only fitting that Moonbeam, Ontario, would greet its visitors with a 5.5-metre-wide flying saucer. But what do folks think when they visit Komarno, Manitoba, for the first time and encounter a giant mosquito with a 4.6-metre wingspan?

A Long Shot

Back in 1992, 22-year-old Jason Zuback walloped a golf ball all the way from the fourth hole tee to the green at the Land-O-Lakes Golf and Country Club in his home town of Coaldale, Alberta. Zuback's ball travelled an amazing 467.26 metres, making him the only player ever to have hit a golf ball that far.

Hitting farther than anyone else in the world is what Zuback does best. In 1996 and 1997 he won the North American Long Drive Championship, and from 1996 to 1999 and in 2006, he was the World Long Drive Champion. A ball hit by Zuback was measured going 336 kilometres per hour. His goal is to hit golf balls as far as is humanly possible.

DID YOU KNOW...

. . . that the longest continually operated company in North America was started in Canada? The Hudson's Bay Company began setting up a chain of trading posts across Canada right after it was founded in 1670, and it's still in business today.

King
of the Dance Floor

From June 28 to July 3, 1983, Alain Dumas danced the days and nights away at a place called the Disco Shop in Granby, Quebec. Nine young women took turns waltzing and two-stepping with him during the non-stop display of his dancing skills. After 120 hours and 30 minutes, Dumas took a bow. He had just established a new individual world record for non-stop ballroom dancing.

DID YOU KNOW...

...that teachers receive more valentines than any other group?

DID YOU KNOW...

. . . that the Anna depicted in the films *The King and I* and *Anna and the King* lived in Canada for nearly forty years? The real Anna was Anna Leonowens, a widowed mother who supported her own two children by teaching the King of Siam's children to speak English. She came to Halifax in 1887, and moved to Montreal 12 years later. She died in Montreal in 1915.

Sharing the Candlelight

Clayton Simko of Windsor was born on February 15, 1994. His sister was delighted. She was born on February 15, so baby Clayton was a great birthday present. Mom was pretty excited about the arrival date too, because February 15 was her birthday as well. And believe it or not, Clayton shared his birthday with his great-grandmother too!

DID YOU KNOW...

. . . that the word CYBERSPACE is the product of the creative Canadian mind of sci-fi writer William Gibson?

Two to One

A football goal post used to look like a giant letter H. Now it looks like a squared off letter Y or a slingshot, thanks to ex-Montreal Alouette coach Jim Trimble and former St. Mary's University coach Bob Hayes. In the mid-sixties, Trimble told Hayes he thought a single-post goal post would work better. It could be set back from the touchdown line, so players wouldn't crash into it as they often did when the two-pole posts were planted on the line.

Hayes liked the idea, made a couple out of scrap metal, and installed them on the St. Mary's field in Halifax. Around the same time, Trimble had an engineer named Cedric Marsh help him design and make a pair of the posts that he gave to the Alouettes to use in 1966. But it wasn't until the new design showed up at the next Orange Bowl game in Miami that pro football movers and shakers realized what an improvement it was. In 1967 the slingshot goal posts scored a touchdown when the National Football League decided they were the only way to go.

DID YOU KNOW...

. . .that every day Canadians devour about 60 million slices of bread? Find that hard to believe? Think sandwiches.

Lining Up to Sign Up

Back in 1942, Carl Lindley of Danville, Illinois, was a long way from home. He was part of a construction team building the Alaska Highway in the Yukon. In a homesick moment, he planted a signpost pointing the way back to Danville. His seedling sign grew into a forest as other visitors to the area followed his example. The World-Famous Signpost Forest of Watson Lake, Yukon, is home to more than 72 000 signs pointing to places all over the globe.

DID YOU KNOW...

. . . that it's illegal to spit on city roads in Kanata, Ontario? The city passed the bylaw in 1999, supposedly to prevent damage to, or hazardous conditions on, the roads. No doubt about it, spitting is gross. But damaging or hazardous? Hmmmmm . . .

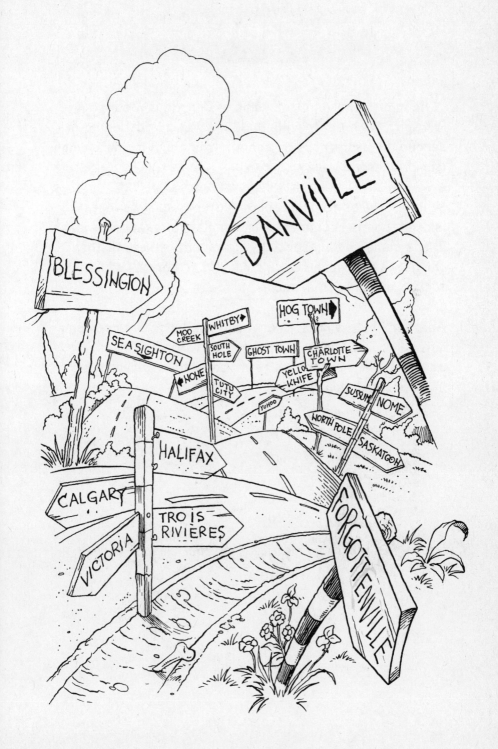

The Name Game

The most common place name in Canada is Mount Pleasant, with Centreville and Lakeview right behind in second. Pleasant pops up again in the third most common name, Pleasant Valley.

When it comes to geographic features such as lakes, islands, ponds and mountains, Long Lake is a clear winner in the name game, especially if you add it in with the third most common feature name, Lac Long. Mud Lake is tucked in between in second place.

Another clear winner emerges in the longest place name category. It's Cape St. George-Petit Jardin-Grand Jardin-De Grau-Marches Point-Loretto, a community in Newfoundland. Yikes!

DID YOU KNOW...

. . . that at least one meteorite of 100 grams or larger thuds into Canadian soil every day? But fewer than five dozen have ever been found because no one is around to hear or see them fall. Apparently, a golf course, with its wide open spaces, is one of the best places to look for them. It would be easier to spot one there than in the woods or in a farmer's field.

Mystery Cake

Christmas fruitcakes aren't as popular as they used to be. The younger crowd doesn't seem willing to give them the respect they deserve. They even make jokes about the same cakes being passed around like hot potatoes from one Christmas to the next. But folks in Manitou Springs, Saskatchewan, make sure that doesn't happen in their community. Each January they hold their Great Fruitcake Toss where they take up bats, golf clubs, slingshots, catapults or anything else that packs a wallop, and send their Christmas cakes sailing through the air.

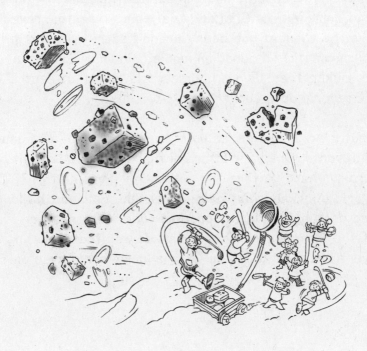

A Lucky Loonie Legend Is Born

Two days after the Canadian women's hockey team won the gold medal at the 2002 Winter Olympics in Salt Lake City, Utah, the men's team did the same. After that game Wayne Gretzky, the team's director, revealed what he thought had been Canada's secret weapon in the tournament — a Canadian loonie coin that Edmonton ice maker Trent Evans had secretly buried at centre ice several days earlier.

That lucky loonie ended up in the Hockey Hall of Fame in Toronto. One year later another lucky loonie went on display there. Before the gold medal game at the 2003 World Championships held in Helsinki, Finland, the loonie had been hidden in the padding under the crossbar of the Swedish team's net. Canada won that game in overtime, and the legend of the lucky loonie lived on!

The loonie was in full view when Canada won silver at the World Junior Hockey Championships in Helsinki in January of 2004. That time it was proudly painted on Canadian goalie Marc-André Fleury's mask as part of the mask's contest-winning design. (The design was submitted by 18-year-old Tanner Klassen of Campbell River, British Columbia.)

$1 Lucky Loonie Again

The loonie itself is lucky to "be alive." Back in 1986, plans were well underway to replace Canada's one-dollar bills with new gold-coloured coins. The new coins were to have a picture of canoe-paddling voyageurs, very similar to the scene depicted on the 1935 silver dollar. In November the master dies — the engraved metal designs that would be used to stamp out the coins — were couriered from Ottawa to the mint in Winnipeg. But, mysteriously, they were lost in transit. Afraid that criminals had stolen them to make counterfeit money, officials chose a brand new design, and the new coins featuring a picture of a loon were introduced in June, 1987. But if the voyageur dies had made it safely to Winnipeg, there would never have been a lucky loonie. And who knows what the new two-dollar coins introduced in 1996 would have been nicknamed!

What's that, eh?

Loonie bin is the nickname Canadians came up with for a piggy bank after the one-dollar coins replaced dollar bills in 1987.

Oh, Borealia, Our Home and Native Land???

How does that sound to you? Does "Oh, Colonia" catch your fancy? Maybe you'd prefer "Transatlantia" or "Britannia"?

These were five of the many suggested names for the new country as plans for Canada's Confederation got underway in the 1860s. Victorialand was also proposed, in honour of Queen Victoria, as was Albertsland, in honour of her husband.

One can understand why Hochelaga and Superior might have been suggested, but why Efisga or Tuponia? Well, look at the first letters of England, France, Ireland, Scotland, Germany and Aboriginal, and you'll see where the idea for Efisga came from. Take the first letters of The United Provinces of North America and you get Tuponia, with the "i" tossed in to make it sound more country-like. And if cooler heads had not prevailed, two other suggestions could have led to Canadians having to introduce themselves as Norlanders or Cabotians.

Just the Stats

On average, Canadians eat 4.4 kilograms of chocolate, in many different shapes and forms, annually. Kit Kats topped the list of favourite chocolate bars in 2003, with Reese's Peanut Butter Cups coming in a close second.

Just the Stats

Vancouver's Capilano suspension bridge is the longest and highest pedestrian suspension bridge in the world. The footbridge stretches 137 metres across the Capilano River canyon and sways 70 metres above it. Crossing it can be a dizzying experience. Some walkers get so nervous they have to turn back part way across.

Prince of the Air

Walking across the Capilano suspension bridge would be a piece of cake for Jay Cochrane, who was born in New Brunswick and grew up in Sudbury, Ontario. He has walked across wires strung high above the ground, and he's been blindfolded when he's done it.

Cochrane is one of the world's greatest funambulists, or tightrope walkers, and he holds several records to prove it. In 1972, he walked a record-setting 4.02 kilometres, travelling back and forth more than 36 metres in the air along a 91.4-metre-long wire stretched between two buildings at the Canadian National Exhibition grounds in Toronto. Thirty-two years later, the 59-year-old was back at the CNE, balancing 20 storeys above the ground as he walked back and forth along a 250-metre-long cable no thicker than his finger.

Cochrane is hugely popular in China, where he managed to accomplish an astonishing funambulism feat. In 1995 he tightrope-walked nearly two-thirds of a kilometre across the Yangtze River, about half a kilometre above the gorge.

DID YOU KNOW...

. . . that Concord Confections in Vaughan, just north of Toronto, is the only company in the world that makes Dubble Bubble bubble gum? The Canadian candy maker has been mixing up and squeezing out tonnes of the popular treat ever since 1998, when it bought Fleer, the company that first came up with the winning formula for Dubble Bubble in 1928.

BIG BITE

If you're looking for a giant energy boost, you could always try to take a bite out of the world's largest perogy, located in Glendon, Alberta. Stabbed through by a huge fork, the massive fibreglass-and-steel dumpling is more than 8 metres high and almost 4 metres wide.

Record-Breaking Bat

Canada's biggest baseball bat towers above the corner of 97th Avenue and 118th Avenue in Edmonton, Alberta. At nearly 16 metres long, this aluminum statue hits a home run in the "biggest tourist attractions" game.

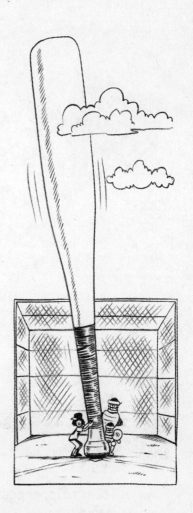

Carry a Big Stick

Duncan, British Columbia, is home to the world's biggest hockey stick and puck. The wood-and-steel stick weighs more than 28 100 kilograms and is 62.5 metres long.

DID YOU KNOW...

. . . that a Canadian holds the world record for throwing a baseball the farthest? Glen Gorbous of Drumheller, Alberta, was a right-armed pitcher who played in the major leagues from 1955–1957. On August 1, 1957, when he was pitching for the Philadelphia Phillies, Gorbous threw a baseball an amazing 135.9 metres!

Just the Stats

The cat that holds the world record for having the most toes was a Canadian. In September, 2002, the Contant family of Bonfield, Ontario, presented their orange tabby, Jake, for an official Guinness World Record check-up. Sure enough, Jake's 28 toes — 7 on each paw — guaranteed him a place in the record books. The previous record holder, a New York cat named Mickey, had just 27 toes. Most cats have 18 — 5 on each front paw, and 4 each on the back ones.

Batter Up at the North Pole

Captain O.C.S. Robertson was one of Canada's finest sailors. In 1954 he was the commanding officer aboard the Canadian navy icebreaker HMCS *Labrador* when it became the first ship ever to sail completely around North America in just one voyage. With plenty of experience sailing through Arctic waters, he was hired by the American navy in 1960 as an ice pilot on the USS *Seadragon* to guide the nuclear submarine through its undersea crossing of the Northwest Passage.

When the submarine surfaced near the North Pole, Robertson decided the sailors needed a break from their cramped quarters, so he organized a baseball game on the ice. He placed first base in the eastern half of the world, and third base in the western hemisphere. With the International Date Line running between first base and home plate, players hitting pop flies across it were caught out the day after they had hit the ball! And runners heading for home were actually making a dash for the North Pole, the place where Robertson had put home plate.

One of a Kind

Early in the morning on January 18, 2000, thousands of people living in the Yukon and Northwest Territories, northern British Columbia and southern Alaska heard what sounded like a huge thunderclap, saw the sky light up as if a giant flashbulb had just gone off, and smelled a sulphury odour in the air. Witnesses reported seeing a massive, multi-coloured fireball plummeting to Earth, leaving behind a glowing orange and blue dust trail that drifted across the sky for about 15 minutes after the fiery explosion. This is how what's come to be known as the Tagish meteorite made its spectacular entry into Earth's atmosphere.

Meteorites are small pieces of space rock that don't burn up upon entry. At least 100 tonnes of them fall to Earth every day, but most are no bigger than specks of dust. The one that landed on Tagish Lake, in northwestern British Columbia, was really big, as meteorites go. It weighed about 200 grams, and more than 500 smaller fragments were collected too. But these bits of space rock might never have been found if Tagish Lake hadn't been frozen when Jim Brook, a local resident, went out on the lake a week later.

Brook was driving home across the ice when he spotted the blackened chunks. He came back the next day, carefully cut out several without touching them with his bare hands, slipped them into plastic bags, brought them home and stored them in his freezer.

The pieces Brook collected would turn out to be the most pristine — or untouched and uncontaminated — meteorites ever found and studied. They would also turn out to be very special in another way. The Tagish meteorite was the very first space rock to have

been identified as coming all the way from a band of asteroids between Mars and Jupiter, about half a billion kilometres away. Researchers will continue to explore the meteor's make-up for years to come, looking for clues to what was going on in the universe so very long ago, when its journey to Earth began.

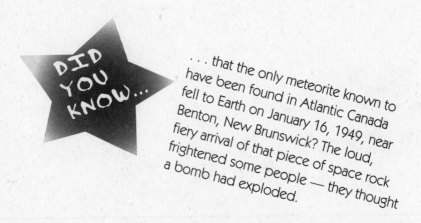

DID YOU KNOW...

. . . that the only meteorite known to have been found in Atlantic Canada fell to Earth on January 16, 1949, near Benton, New Brunswick? The loud, fiery arrival of that piece of space rock frightened some people — they thought a bomb had exploded.

BOOM!

Band of Fool's Gold

Wildlife workers regularly put metal bands around the legs of migratory birds to track where they go each spring and fall. The bands have numbers on them, and anyone finding a banded bird — dead or alive — is encouraged to report where it was found. Experts studying the birds will often pay a small reward to anyone who takes the time to pass on that information.

These inexpensive bands and the money paid for reporting them are most likely what first inspired a bored prankster or an inventive storyteller to come up with the idea late in the winter of 2001. But once started, the rumour spread quickly around Arivat, Nunavut, and to several other hamlets in the area — a snow goose had been released wearing a band of gold worth a million dollars!

Folks were skeptical when they first heard about the gold ring, but it was a good story, so they passed it on . . . and on . . . and on. Eventually Canadian Wildlife Services started getting phone calls from people wanting to know if it was true. Officials said it wasn't, but since the spring migration had begun, they wondered if more hunters than usual would be taking aim at the returning snow geese. After all, a chance to make a million bucks would be hard to ignore. But a quick investigation showed that hunters weren't shooting more geese. They may have liked the story, but they were too smart to fall for the hoax.

Where did you say?

Thunder Bay, Ontario, isn't a stormy place, as the name might suggest. The city at the head of Lake Superior is actually named after the thunderbird, a powerful figure in many aboriginal legends and myths.

DID YOU KNOW...

. . . that the site of Regina, Saskatchewan, was once called Pile o' Bones? It was named for the buffalo bones left behind after Cree hunters had removed the meat and skins.

What's that, eh?

"Holy" dollars circulated briefly in Prince Edward Island in the early 1800s. They weren't holy in any religious sense, but they were holey, explaining why locals gave them the "holy" nickname.

A shortage of coins had been a problem in P.E.I. for many years when Lieutenant-Governor Charles Smith arrived there in 1813. To make it easier for people to buy and sell goods, Smith came up with a two-for-one plan. He had the centres punched out of Spanish silver dollars. The outer rings would still be worth the coin's full value, and the doughnut-hole middles would be worth a shilling (about 10 cents).

It didn't take counterfeiters long to spot the plan's major flaw — the two new coins were worth more than the original one. They started punching out dollars on their own, increasing their personal buying power and keeping the added value from the government. The plan was short-lived and the holey holy dollars were quickly taken out of circulation.

Sneaky, Sneaky . . .

One of the wackiest, but workable, ideas in shipping history was cooked up in Canada. A man named C.M.R. McPherson came up with the idea to avoid paying new taxes that Britain had started collecting on pine and oak timber exported from Canada in the 1820s. He designed a cargo ship that could, in effect, be used to smuggle out taxable timber right under the watchful eyes of port officials. How? By building a disposable ship! It would be built with large, squared-off logs pegged together in such a way that they could easily be taken apart when the ship reached England.

Two such ships were built in Quebec City. The first sailed from Quebec in 1824, but it wasn't taken apart as planned when it arrived in England. It returned to Canada to pick up more cargo, and sank on its second voyage across the Atlantic. However, the second ship was broken up when it made it to Britain, without a cent of export tax being paid on the timbers when they were sold.

Oops, we're sorry

In 2000, Nova Scotia's tourism bureau proudly released a new official map of the province, but pride soon changed to embarrassment. Pictou — the only town in the riding of John Hamm, premier of the province at the time — had been left off the map. When word of the error became public, red-faced officials rushed out to get some "Pictou" stickers printed, and government workers carefully pasted them in the correct location.

Oooops,
we're really,
really sorry

It's bad enough to omit one town from a provincial map. But what about leaving a third of one province, all of another one, an entire territory, and the largest freshwater lake in the world, off a map of Canada? You'd probably fail a geography test if you slipped up like that.

The Canadian Tourism Commission definitely flunked out with the public and the media when it did that and more. The Commission meant well. It was the summer of 2003, and tourists were afraid of catching SARS (severe acute respiratory syndrome). So officials decided to help attract visitors, especially from the United States, by putting out a travel guide and a glossy magazine called *PureCanada*, featuring interesting places to go and fun things to do. But when the new promotional material was distributed — all 270 000 copies — embarrassed Commission staff had a bit of explaining to do. The maps in both the guide and the magazine were, to put it mildly, incomplete.

Nunavut, Canada's newest territory, had been misspelled as Nunavit, and Halifax and Fredericton — two provincial capitals — weren't on the maps. Neither were Brandon, Manitoba, and most of northwestern Ontario. And Prince Edward Island, Yukon Territory and Lake Superior had disappeared too.

The best the Commission could come up with was a promise to get things right in the second edition of *PureCanada*, scheduled to come out later that year.

Bright Idea

When city councillors in Calgary voted to replace nearly 50 000 200-watt streetlights with 100-watt bulbs in the summer of 2001, they didn't do it just to save energy. The switch also cut down on light pollution. Astronomers were pleased, telescope users were happy, and kids were delighted. On a clear night they could see the Milky Way again.

DID YOU KNOW...

. . . that peewee curlers in Canada play in Little Rock leagues, and are nicknamed "Little Rockers"? Curling's popularity has been growing steadily over the last several years, and there are now at least 1.3 million curlers in Canada. The game was first played here by Scottish soldiers in 1789.

Rock On!

Slithering into Spring

Each spring, thousands of visitors are drawn to Narcisse, Manitoba, as soon as the last snow has melted. What brings them to this small town about 150 kilometres north of Winnipeg isn't everyone's idea of a great tourist attraction. But the area around Narcisse is home to the largest number of over-wintering red-sided garter snakes in the world, and when up to 50 000 of them emerge from their underground dens, or hibernacula, they are definitely a sight to behold.

After hibernating for seven months, waves of males slither out of cracks in the limestone and wait for the females to emerge. When the females appear, the males swarm all over them, twisting themselves into tangled, seething clumps called mating balls. After they mate, the snakes unravel and slip away in search of their first big meal of the season. Late in September, the ground seethes with life again as the snakes migrate back to their dens about 2 metres below the surface.

The chance to take in this spectacular show is what brings the crowds to Narcisse, especially in the spring. For a few weeks each year the snakes have star billing, winning over even the most ophidiophobic — that's "fearful of snakes" to most of us — members of their audience.

Reptile Invaders

Students attending school in Alonsa, Manitoba, in the 1990s didn't need to go on field trips to Narcisse to watch garter snakes come out of hibernation each spring. The snakes came to them, and more than a few of the students and teachers weren't thrilled to see them.

The problem started when the snakes returned to their home one September and found themselves locked out. For years they'd been hibernating in the basement of an old building near the school, but the building's owner had decided to seal off their den. So the snakes slithered around until they found another cozy place to spend the winter — Alonsa's school. Slipping through cracks in the basement wall, hundreds of them moved in and settled down for the winter.

Come spring, they were on the move again, slithering through the air vents and across the ceilings, looking for a way out. Just hearing them squirming around was enough to upset the more squeamish students, but nearly everyone, teachers included, found it hard to cope with them dropping down from vents and slip-sliding along bookshelves. A wildlife expert came to the rescue, collecting most of the reptilian visitors and taking them away to more suitable locations. But when September rolled around, they were back.

Repairing the foundations helped, but a few persistent snakes still managed to sneak into the building, and many of them kept hanging out in the playground each spring and fall. After a few years, conservationists finally convinced them to relocate to a new den built just for them north of the school property. But it took a while for some students to stop wondering what else they'd get when they pulled a book off a library shelf.

Walter

the Famous Farting Dog

Back in the 1970s and '80s Beverly Delong's pet
bull mastiff, Walter, had quite the reputation in
Fredericton, New Brunswick. He wasn't well-known
because he did heroic things like rescuing drowning
children or hunting down bank robbers. He was no
fighter either. No, Walter's fame grew because he
could empty a room faster than a cry of "Fire!" just by
passing gas — something he did with great regularity.

Walter's silent but deadly emissions were legendary, and
tales of his "problem" lingered in the Fredericton air
long after he had gone to doggy heaven. Glenn Murray, a
local educator familiar with Walter's famed flatulence,
eventually decided to write a picture book about it.
For ten years, though, publishers kept rejecting his
manuscript, certain that the smelly subject matter
would doom the book to failure. But in 1999, Murray and
American author William Kotzwinkle joined forces to

WALTER
THE
SCRATCH
'N'
SNIFF
EDITION

produce a version of Walter's story that a publisher liked. *Walter the Farting Dog*, illustrated by Audrey Colman, hit bookstores in 2001, and was soon flying off the shelves. It was on the *New York Times'* bestseller list for most of 2003, and by April of 2004 the book had sold half a million copies.

A sequel, *Walter the Farting Dog: Trouble at the Garage Sale*, followed in the spring of 2004, much to the delight of Beverly Delong, by then a school principal in Fredericton. She was happy to see that once kids got to know him, they loved the fictional Walter as much as she had loved her real-life pet in spite of his "problem." And Glenn Murray is delighted too. Thanks to Walter's skyrocketing popularity, he's enjoying the sweet smell of success.

Another Smelly Success Story

Glenn Murray isn't the only Canadian writer to have had trouble trying to get a story about gas-passing published. None other than bestselling children's author Robert Munsch ran into similar difficulties trying to find a home for one of his stories. Youngsters loved hearing him tell the tale, but editors figured a book called *The Fart* would never sell. Finally, Doubleday

Canada accepted the story, but insisted on a title change. Munsch came up with a new one — *Good Families Don't* — and another bestseller was born.

But when most kids go looking for that story in a library or bookstore, they usually just ask for "the fart book by Robert Munsch." They get a real kick out of saying the word publishers shied away from, and judging from sales, they love seeing it in print too. Fart, fart, fart, fart . . .

Faithful to the End

Torontonian Meryl Dunsmore received the first mysterious valentine card in the mail in 1928, when she was 16. Signed "Your secret admirer," it offered no clues as to who the sender might be. Meryl wondered if it was from a shy boy who had a crush on her in high school, but she really had no idea who had sent it . . . or the one that arrived the next year . . . or the year after that.

February after February the cards kept coming, even after Meryl had left home, married, remarried and moved six times. Often the cards were mailed from other countries such as France, China, Australia, South Africa and Japan, but they were always signed in the same handwriting from either "Your secret admirer" or "Your secret pal."

When February, 1968, passed without a card arriving, Meryl and her husband, Alex, couldn't help wondering about what might have happened to the mysterious romantic.

That summer, they found out. A card arrived in July, with a brief note apologizing for missing Valentine's Day because the sender had been ill.

The cards kept coming for another 20 years. The one that arrived in 1988 was the first one sent from Sweden. The verse inside read simply: "An old fashioned wish is always in style, when it comes from the heart, and is sent with a smile."

That was the last message from her anonymous admirer that Meryl would read, but it was not the last one he would send. Meryl died in July 1988. The morning of her funeral, a bouquet of white lilies and yellow mums appeared mysteriously on the steps of the funeral home. There were just five words on the unsigned card attached to the flowers: "Rest in peace, my Valentine."

With love from
– er – L❂ve

Come February, thoughts turn to Love. And that's *Love* with a capital *L*, as in the name of a small village about 20 kilometres north of Nipawin, Saskatchewan, just west of Tobin Lake. Fewer than 100 people live in Love, but just before Valentine's Day each year, business really picks up at the local post office. Hundreds of envelopes mailed to the postmaster start arriving from across Canada and around the world. Inside the envelopes are more envelopes containing Valentine cards or notes. Each one is sealed, stamped, addressed and ready to be mailed as soon as it receives a cancellation postmark from Love.

What better way to show you care than to send your love to your true love from Love?

BUSYBODY BEAVERS

There were millions and millions of beavers in Canada 400 years ago, but by the 1930s they had disappeared from many parts of the country. So conservationists began reintroducing pairs of *Castor canadensis* in those areas and let nature take its course.

Nature was kind, and with no bears or wolves to prey on the beavers in farming and urban areas, their population grew and grew. By the 1990s in Manitoba, for instance, beaver numbers had soared from the hundreds to the hundreds of thousands. But one beaver can gnaw down more than 200 trees a year, so wherever beaver numbers are going up, lots of trees are coming down. That wouldn't be a problem in the wilderness, but in and near cities, it is. In Calgary, for example, they've taken a liking to the trees in some parks. Persistent dam-builders have also driven some

Prairie farmers to sell their land by turning fields into flooded swamps.

So, the good news is that the *Castor canadensis* population is thriving now. The bad news — for the beavers — is that there's now a price on their heads in some parts of Canada. It seems the country's national animal is becoming a national pest.

3-
2-
1-
Leap!

In 1979, Toronto's CN Tower was the site of the highest stunt fall ever made for a movie. Ace American stuntman Dar Robinson made the leap, plunging from the 335-metre-high Lookout level of the tower. About 91 metres from the ground, Robinson released a hidden parachute that opened just in time to break his fall. Robinson's stunt, performed as actor Christopher Plummer's double, was featured in a film called *Highpoint*.

. . . that Nana, the children's canine nanny in the novel Peter Pan, was a Newfoundland dog, not a St. Bernard as shown in the Disney animated film?

WOOF!

Great balls of.... plastic wrap?

Well, there was one ball of the clingy wrap at a Toronto restaurant back in 2003. Andy Martell, a cook at Scratch Danial's, started forming the wrap into a ball just for the fun of it. By the time he'd had enough, he'd come up with a record-breaker. The ball measured nearly 140 centimetres around and weighed more than 20 kilos, and could lay claim to being the largest ball of plastic wrap in the world.

CBC vs. the Beavers

Saskatchewan grain farmer Tom Harper spent the summer of 2002 battling some very busy beavers. Each night the beavers would stuff branches into a culvert, or large pipe, near his house. With the pipe blocked, the creek that ran through it would back up, threatening to flood his home. Each morning, Harper would unplug the culvert, but each night the beavers would be back at work.

Harper tried to get a conservation officer to trap and relocate them, but was told that would cost too much. He shot a couple, but hated doing that; besides, replacement workers were soon back on the job. One night, though, when he was out trying to stop them, he noticed that his yelling and muttering made them back off a little. That's when he got the brainwave about the radio. He brought one outside, tuned in a CBC station that features lots of talking, and turned up the volume. After two weeks, the beavers surrendered and moved on.

Harper's victory was featured on a TV news show. The CTV reporter who interviewed him figured viewers might get a kick out of hearing that Harper's secret weapon against Canada's national animal was Canada's national broadcaster, the CBC.

AND NOW FOR YOUR LOCAL FORECAST...

What's that, eh?

If you go ice skating on the Rideau Canal in Ottawa, you're bound to come across beaver tails. They're warm, sweet-smelling and delicious, and have nothing to do with the busy, dam-building rodents' tails except for the fact that both are flat, rounded at one end and thinner at the other. Beaver tails are popular pastries that vendors sell from booths scattered along the shores of the canal. They're also sold in many bakeries across Canada.

A taste-testing bite will tell you that a beaver tail is really just a yeast-type doughnut that isn't shaped like one. It is usually coated in icing sugar or plain white sugar right after it comes out of the frying oil, but it is also served spread with jam or coated with maple syrup.

Ride On!

The Canadian Horse is the oldest breed of horse in Canada. The first one was shipped to Canada from France in 1647. Two more stallions and 12 mares arrived in New France 18 years later, and a century after that, there were about 12 000 of their offspring on Canadian soil. Although smaller than many other breeds of workhorses, the Canadian proved to be tough, strong and well-behaved. Settlers rode them and used them to clear and plow their land and to pull their carriages and sleighs. The breed nearly died out in the early 1900s, but careful planning and financial support from Ottawa has now guaranteed its survival.

On April 30, 2002, Parliament officially named the Canadian Horse as a national symbol of the country, right up there with the beaver and the maple leaf.

A Brave Breed

Newfoundland dogs are named after the province where they were first spotted by Vikings as far back as 1000 CE. Usually black, they're big, gentle creatures who aren't afraid of hard work. They're also perfectly suited to life at sea. Since water rolls off their oily coats and their webbed feet make them superb swimmers, they have often braved the icy Atlantic to rescue people from drowning. Boatswain was one such rescuer, and his efforts actually changed the course of history.

A British navy captain brought Boatswain to England in 1801, when he was just a pup. Thirteen years and several VIP owners later, Boatswain was again in the care of an English navy captain whose ship was anchored off the west coast of Italy, close to the island of Elba. One stormy night a political prisoner living in exile on Elba managed to board the British ship in the hope of escaping back to France. As his supporters worked to secure the ship, the prisoner — who couldn't swim — slipped off the deck into the murky sea. Boatswain was the only one who saw the man fall, and in a flash, he had leapt in after him, holding him above the waves until sailors could rescue him. The man Boatswain rescued that night was the French emperor Napoleon, who lived to escape and fight another day.

So, if a Newfoundland dog hadn't saved Napoleon that evening in 1814, would he have lived to battle Britain's Admiral Nelson and "meet his Waterloo" in 1815?

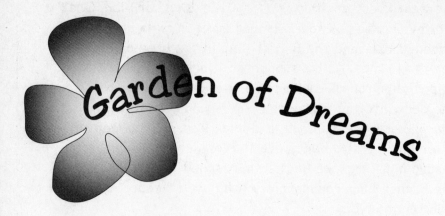

Garden of Dreams

When Canadian soldier Ernest Wilbur Johnstone returned home to Prince Edward Island after World War I, he couldn't forget the striking beauty of the many gardens and parks he had seen in Britain. So he bought a piece of farmland (known locally as the Woodleigh property) near Kensington, and set about trying to transplant some of that beauty to his island home.

Ernest had quite the green thumb, and after years of hard work he made his dream come true. He had surrounded his home with hectare after hectare of lush rolling lawns, shimmering pools and fabulous flowers, shrubs and trees. But after he and his son, Archie, returned from overseas service in World War II, he decided that a few stately buildings were just what his gardens needed to give them an added British flavour.

With Archie's help, Wilbur started building castles and cathedrals. Stone by stone, father and son assembled amazingly detailed mini-replicas of such famous British landmarks as St. Paul's Cathedral, Dunvegan Castle, Yorkminster Cathedral and parts of the Tower of London. Some sections of several of the small buildings were big enough to move around in. Each one took years to complete. Yorkminster Cathedral, Woodleigh-style, was a five-year effort lovingly fitted with thousands of jewel-bright panes of stained glass fitted into its 145 windows. The Tower of London took nine years to finish.

People from across P.E.I. started dropping by to view the structures, and eventually the Johnstones realized that their private dream had become very public. In 1958, Woodleigh Replicas opened as a tourist attraction. Nearly fifty years later, visitors continue to drop by to marvel at what Ernest Johnstone created.

Squeeeeeeeeeeeeeeeeeeeeeeze!

According to the 2004 *Guinness World Records Book*, the skinniest commercial building in the world is in Vancouver. Known as the Sam Kee Building, it's located on West Pender Street in Vancouver's thriving Chinatown district. The land on which it stands is part of a 9-metre-deep piece of property once owned by Chang Toy and Shum Moon, two very successful businessmen who owned the Sam Kee Company.

In 1912 the city made the men sell a 7-metre-deep strip of their land as part of a project to widen Pender Street. That left Toy and Moon just a 2-metre-deep section that the city thought the men would give up because it was too thin to do anything with. When Toy asked to be paid for the remaining land, the city refused, so he decided to make the best of it. His company put up a two-storey building less than 2 metres deep and just over 29 metres long. The ground floor housed shops and offices and the second floor was an apartment. In the basement, along the length of the building and stretching out under the street, Toy had public baths built.

Toy died in 1920, but his very mini strip mall still stands today and is a popular stop for tourists walking through Vancouver's Chinatown.

2 metres

Bow WOW!

Dogs in North Vancouver must be the smartest canines in the world. They don't just jump, heel, fetch and roll over. Apparently, they can read too. Why else would a sign reminding their owners of the "poop and scoop" bylaw, also include the following words:

ATTENTION, DOGS:

GRRRR, BARK, WOOF.

GOOD DOG.

Just the Stats

Every year dogs bite more than 450 000 Canadians. (There are no reliable statistics on how many Canadians bite dogs each year.)

Rock ON!

On January 11, 2003, Avril Lavigne became the youngest musician ever to reach Number 1 on the United Kingdom's top album chart. On the day her best-selling album *Let Go* topped the charts, the pop star from Napanee, Ontario, was just 18 years and 106 days old.

On November 19, 2011, another Canadian music sensation, Justin Bieber of Stratford, Ontario, became the first ever solo artist to have not just one, but three Number 1 albums in the UK and three in the United States — all before he was 18. Bieber was still just 17 when *My World 2.0*, *Never Say Never: The Remixes* and *Under the Mistletoe* all enjoyed top billing. And by early February, 2013, with *Boyfriend* sales skyrocketing, Bieber became the first musical artist ever to have five Number 1 albums before turning 19.

In 2013, award-winning rapper, Drake, from Toronto, Ontario, became the first musical artist to have twelve Number 1 singles on *Billboard* magazine's Hot Rap Songs chart. He also had ten singles — more than any other rapper — on top of *Billboard's* Hot Rhythm and Blues/Hip-Hop Songs chart.

. . . that from 2001 to 2009 Aubrey Graham, the actor who played basketball star Jimmy Brooks on the TV series *Degrassi: The Next Generation* was the rising rap star Drake, whose full name is Aubrey Drake Graham, was also the voice of Ethan, the handsome woolly mammoth that Peaches really liked, in the 2012 animated film, *Ice Age: Continental Drift.*

. . . On March 14, 2011, hundreds of adoring fans crowded in front of a glass display case holding the newest acquisition of Toronto's Bata Shoe Museum — a reddish pair of size seven high top sneakers worn by Justin Bieber in 2010.

A Corner Fit for a Queen

When Queen Elizabeth II visited Iqaluit, the capital of Nunavut, in October of 2002, she did something she'd never done before — she unveiled a street sign. Getting a new street sign isn't usually a big deal, but this sign was Iqaluit's first, so Her Majesty did the honours at the corner of Miwik Avenue and a street called Queen Elizabeth II Way.

One of the most honoured women in Canada was known simply as "the nurse." Myra Grimsley was 29 when she came from England in 1921 to work as a nurse on the west coast of Newfoundland's northern peninsula. Planning to stay for just 2 years, she married a local man named Angus Bennett in 1922 and spent the next 50 years helping people who lived in isolated hamlets there.

Because the nearest doctor was often 100 or more kilometres away, nurse Bennett was often the only person around with any medical expertise. During her long career, she pulled 3000 teeth and delivered 5000 babies — the last one her own grandson. Once, when her brother-in-law's foot was nearly completely cut off in a sawmill accident, she cleaned the wound, numbed it with snow, and sewed the foot back to his ankle. Then she and her husband set out on a perilous three-day journey by dogsled to get her patient to a doctor. When the doctor saw Bennett's stitching, he left it alone, telling the nurse he couldn't have done any better himself. Her re-attachment was so successful that her brother-in-law was eventually able to walk again.

Bennett received many honours, including an honorary doctorate from Memorial University, for her tireless efforts in Newfoundland. She was also awarded the King George V Jubilee Medal, both the King George VI and Queen Elizabeth II Coronation medals, an Order of the British Empire medal, and the Order of Canada. Bennett died in 1990, when she was 100 years old.

Feeding the Imagination
[or Nothing Cheesy About It]

Montreal artist Cosimo Cavallaro's work has included photographs, films, videos and large steel sculptures. But it's his work with cheese — yes, cheese — that has attracted the most publicity.

Cavallaro likes cheese. He sees it as milk, a source of life. After moving to New York City in 1995, he started thinking about "painting" with cheese. He coated a fashion model in it and decorated a hotel room with it. But his biggest cheese piece was an entire house in Powell, Wyoming. In the fall of 2001, he began spraying the vacant house with

5 tonnes of warm, melted pepperjack cheese. The cheese dripped from the ceilings, coated the walls and covered the furniture. It was a sight to behold . . . and to smell, too. The house was demolished a few weeks later, but not before eager visitors had lined up to tour it and TV crews had showed up to capture footage of it for the evening news.

Another Canadian artist, Jana Sterbak, turned to a food item for one of her works of art. In 1991 she made a dress from 22 kilograms of salted, raw flank steak. She photographed a model wearing the beef outfit, and placed that picture beside the dress when it was displayed on a hanger at the National Gallery in Ottawa. Then she left the dress to rot. Some gallery visitors didn't appreciate her vivid reminder of the aging process and decay and the foolishness of paying too much attention to one's physical appearance. Sterbak's art upset vegetarians, and a few meat eaters saw the piece as a waste of food, but it certainly gave everyone who saw it something to think about. Sterbak replaced the decaying piece with a new dress every six weeks.

Shooting Stars

When it came to playing basketball, no team did it better than the Edmonton Grads. A women's team formed in Edmonton in 1915, the Grads absolutely ruled their sport until they disbanded in 1940. Time and again they won city, provincial and Canadian championships; they also represented Canada at the Olympic Games in 1924, 1928, 1932 and 1936.

Because women's basketball was just an exhibition sport, not an official Olympic event until 1976, the Grads never brought home any Olympic medals, but their efforts were golden. They won all 27 of their exhibition matches at the Olympics, and outscored teams from other countries by a total of 1863 points to 297! In a game against a team from Paris, for instance, they won 109-20, and they slaughtered a team from London by a score of 100-2. In all, the 38 women who played for the Grads over the years chalked up an incredible 502 wins. Of the 20 games they did lose, many were exhibition matches played against men's teams. It was the Grads' many triumphs, not Wayne Gretzky's Oilers', which earned Edmonton the honour of being known as the City of Champions.

FANtastic!

Brandy Elliott must have really wanted to see Elton John perform in Saskatoon in August of 2002. Why else would she have spent an entire weekend chasing after grasshoppers? That's what you had to do to have any hope of winning a contest a Regina radio station decided to run. The grand prize — two tickets to the pop star's concert — would go to the listener who brought in the most of those crop-eating, ditch-hopping, juice-spitting insects.

Eager to win the tickets, Elliott started collecting grasshoppers — never in short supply in Saskatchewan — by hand. Fingers stained and back aching, the 26-year-old soon realized she'd have to improve her trapping technique. Using pieces of screening, she made three big nets, attached them to her truck, and started driving along the shoulders and ditches of a country road. As the startled hoppers jumped and flew up, the nets scooped them up by the hundreds.

Elliott collected several pails of the bugs this way, and when her total was calculated, the radio station announced she had won. Another listener had turned in 33 000 grasshoppers, but Elliott had caught 39 000. The concert tickets were hers.

YES to YUCK!

Buckley's Mixture, the famous cough medicine, is a Canadian concoction. Toronto pharmacist William Knapp Buckley worked out the formula for the yucky-tasting stuff back in 1919 during a terrible flu epidemic, and started marketing it a year later.

Buckley realized early on how important advertising was. He was one of the first business owners to start using radio ads to spread the word about his product across Canada. In the 1930s, he introduced Americans to his cough syrup. Like his Canadian customers, they found it soothing, but weren't impressed with its taste. But Buckley believed in his mixture and wouldn't change the ingredients.

In the 1940s, Buckley's son Frank joined the family business. He was the one responsible for an award-winning advertising campaign in the 1980s that dared to have as its slogan, "It tastes awful. And it works." And he personally appeared in TV spots, saying with a straight face, "I wake up with nightmares that someone gives me a taste of my own medicine." Even if people didn't like Buckley's, they really enjoyed the refreshing blend of honesty and humour the company brought to those ads. W. K. Buckley Ltd. still takes that approach in its commercials. Like the claim made for its bad-tasting mixture, it works.

Scarecrow Invasion

Scarecrows have been invading Meaford, Ontario, every October since 1997. As part of a harvest festival, residents stuff, dress and pose them throughout the town. Some folks also dress up as scarecrows to dance, march and stroll in the parade that's always a festival highlight. In 2002, a world-record-breaking 2043 scarecrows leaned against lampposts, sat on benches, balanced on bicycles, rested on ladders and peeked out of windows, much to the delight of the crowds of tourists who came to check them out.

Feathered Friends – NOT!

A collection of geese is called a gaggle, a group of lions is called a pride, and a gathering of crows is called a murder. And murder is what some of the 35 000 residents of Woodstock, Ontario, had in mind when way too many crows moved into town in 2002 — about 20 000 of them, by some estimates. They cawed non-stop as they fought over food they had ripped out of garbage bags, or glared down from trees at nervous passersby. They splattered a thick, foul-smelling layer of droppings on cars, decks and patio furniture, driving many people out of their backyards that summer. And, every now and then, one of the more aggressive ones swooped down like a diving bomber and attacked a person.

At sunset another 20 000 or so of the crows' country relatives would fly in from surrounding farms, noisily jostling for space on telephone wires, branches and roofs. Darkness brought silence, but not much relief, because everyone knew that the birds were still lurking in the shadows, hunched down on their perches, just waiting for the crack of dawn. Then, they would take off in an explosion of noise, at least two hours before most people needed to wake up. The nightmare was never-ending. In the fall, people desperate for a good night's sleep and fed up with washing off bird poop demanded that city officials take action. So the council hired Martin Wernaart, a professional crow-scarer, to drive off the birds. After weeks of shooting off flare guns that lit up the sky and filled the air with loud pops and whistling sounds, Wernaart managed to convince many of the crows to get out of town.

Chatham, Ontario, suffered through a similar invasion in the late 1990s. By the fall of 2000, nearly 225 000 crows were tormenting its residents. But by January, 2001, fewer than 200 remained. Chathams's solution was to hire a company that brought in trained falcons, hawks and eagles to circle above the city for several days. Workers also walked around with a few great horned owls perched securely on their arms. Clever birds that they are, the crows got the message — leave town or become lunch for their natural enemies. They took off.

Snow Day — NOT!

Canadian kids usually cheer when a major snowstorm shuts down schools. But when a blizzard battered the community of St. Anthony, Newfoundland, late in February of 2003, 47 youngsters didn't. Instead of getting the day off, they got stuck at school.

With drifts more than 3 metres high piling up against the doors and windows, only those children who lived in town could make it home in time. So for two days the rest of the students and the staff had to bunk down in classrooms, and eat whatever could be cooked up in the school kitchen. But the kids did get to play games and watch movies with their friends, things they might not have been able to do if they'd been snowed in at home. At least they had some fun, thanks to the efforts of the 29 staff members who probably couldn't wait to hear that the snowplows had finished clearing the roads.

DID YOU KNOW...

. . . that smoking on the street was banned in Quebec for nearly 100 years, from the 1670s to the 1750s? The penalty for public puffing was a whipping with a cat-o'-nine-tails. Public flirting was also a no-no for several years. The daughter of Lieutenant-Governor Pierre André was actually sent back to France in 1736 when she was caught batting her eyelashes and flashing a smile at a handsome fellow on the street.

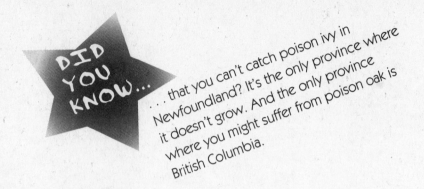

. . . that you can't catch poison ivy in Newfoundland? It's the only province where it doesn't grow. And the only province where you might suffer from poison oak is British Columbia.

Mind If I Have a Look?

Voyageur Alexis Bidagan, known as Alexis St. Martin, made one of the most important contributions to the modern medical study of human digestion.

St. Martin didn't want to become a famous human guinea pig, but that's what happened after he received a horrific shotgun wound that blew away a large part of his chest in 1822. Dr. William Beaumont, an American army surgeon, treated St. Martin as best he could, but declared that the man wouldn't survive.

Miraculously, however, St. Martin did survive, but he was left with an open wound in his side that lined up with a hole in his stomach that never healed. These two holes served as a window into his digestive tract, one that Beaumont couldn't resist looking through. Some people thought he could have done more to close the wound; instead, he spent two years caring for St. Martin as he was, and then hired him so he could readily see what happened to the food and drink that passed through St. Martin's stomach.

Toilet Trap

In August, 2002, little Aidin Richard of Riverview, New Brunswick, wasn't potty-trained yet, but he was curious about how toilets worked. Playing in the toilet was a definite no-no, but one day he found the urge to do so irresistible. Fortunately for him, the toilet he decided to explore was new and hadn't been fully installed yet. Unfortunately for him, when he tried to stuff a huge wad of toilet paper into the bowl, his arm got stuck in the hole at the bottom of it. After a few minutes trying to pull his arm out, he did what any curious but frightened two-year-old would do in a similar fix — he started screaming his head off.

His mother, Shannon, came running to help, but Aidin's arm had swelled up and she couldn't budge it. So she did what any frantic mother with a child trapped in a toilet would do — she called the fire department. When the firefighters arrived, they carefully examined Aidin's predicament. Then they did what any self-respecting, well-trained firefighters would do — they whacked the toilet bowl with a hammer. When it cracked apart, Aidin's hand popped free. Aidin, his mother and the firefighters all recovered quickly from the traumatic episode. The damage to the toilet proved to be fatal.

Dinosaur Poop

In 1995, staff from the Royal Saskatchewan Museum were busy excavating "Scotty," the nickname given to a *Tyrannosaurus rex* skeleton discovered in 1991 near the town of Eastend, about 150 kilometres southwest of Swift Current. It was just a couple of kilometres from the skeleton site that museum worker Wendy Sloboda made another amazing find — the biggest coprolite, or fossilized dung, that scientists are certain came from a large theropod, or carnivorous dinosaur, most likely a *T. rex*.

As coprolites go, this one was really big — about 44 by 16 by 13 centimetres. About 200 other small pieces of the original "deposit" were found nearby. Add them all up, and you've got a piece of dinosaur poop that would have been about 2.4 litres in volume 65 million years ago.

Scientists can learn a lot about the diets of prehistoric animals by studying the contents of fossilized feces. After analyzing bone fragments imbedded in this king-sized coprolite, researchers concluded that a *T. rex* had most likely dined on a younger, smaller dinosaur about as big as a cow, crunching it up bones and all. Chalk up another first for Canada. It's home to the biggest known piece of dinosaur poop in the world.

... that the dark red, sweet-smelling Spartan apple is Canadian? It's a cross between a Newton Pippin and another world-famous Canadian apple, the McIntosh. The Spartan was bred and first successfully grown in British Columbia in the 1930s.

Happy Faces All Around

Montreal is very serious about fun and laughter, so much so that it's home to a museum honouring the important role that humour has played in people's lives. The Just for Laughs Museum is no joke. Nor is the Juste pour rire/Just for Laughs Festival. Held annually since 1983, it attracts hundreds of big-name comedians from around the world, all very serious about trying to make Montrealers and visitors to the city laugh for days on end.

Big Star
Bigger Co-star

Actress Fay Wray, best remembered for her 1933 *King Kong* role as the screaming blond beauty trapped in the clutches of the giant ape atop a New York City skyscraper, was born near Cardston, Alberta, in 1907. Eighty-six years later, in September, 1993, Cardston residents welcomed back their favourite hometown girl, throwing a big party in her honour. Wray died in New York in August 2004 at age 96.

What's that, eh?

Poutine had become so popular by the early 2000s that many fast food restaurants across Canada started adding it to their menus. Fernand Lachance of Warwick, Quebec, claimed the honour of being the first to come up with the yummy-tasting, calorie-loaded gooey combo of cheese curds and french fries in his restaurant back in 1957. He would heap both into a plastic bag so customers could take the concoction with them. Later on, at the request of a customer, he added gravy to the mix, and locals loved it.

Poutine's popularity eventually spread across the province, and visitors to Quebec often made a point of finding a restaurant that served it. By the 1990s, the dish was being cooked up in homes and restaurants far beyond Quebec's borders. Now it's known as a distinctly Canadian food item. Dietitians may not approve of its high fat and calorie content, but in the Great White North, it has become one of life's guilty pleasures. Many visitors to the country are also guilty of giving in to its gooey charm.

No Eruptions Here, Eh?

Contrary to some claims, Montreal is NOT built around a volcanic mountain. True, Mount Royal is made of igneous rock — hot melted rock, or magma, that cooled and hardened again. But that magma never made it up to the earth's surface from an active volcano. It worked its way up from the Earth's core, pushing up the rock above it into small mountains and hills like Mount Royal. Over millions of years, the surface rock wore away, leaving the igneous rock exposed and making some people think the Mount must have once been a volcano.

DID YOU KNOW...

... that in 1854, when they were trying to halt the spread of cholera, Quebec City officials forbade all burials within the city limits?

Very Special Delivery

Like Stanley in the children's books by the late Jeff Brown, Flat Mark was as flat as the paper he was made of. To honour Brown's delightful character, Grade 4 students at Fenside Public School in Toronto made Flat Mark after reading *Flat Stanley* with their teacher, Karlo Cabrera. They also made some flat snacks and a flat coat for Flat Mark, because he was about to go on a trip. Then they wrote a letter explaining why they were sending Flat Mark away, slipped it and Mark into a large envelope, addressed it and put it in the mail. They were hoping that the person who received him would take the time to write back, telling them about some of the things Mark saw during his visit.

The person the students had decided to have Flat Mark visit in November of 2003 was Paul Martin, the new leader of the Liberal Party, who was about to become prime minister. Their teacher expected nothing more than a brief letter and a photograph back from Martin, figuring that he could use these to introduce his students to a unit on government. But Cabrera and his students got much, much more.

When Flat Mark arrived in Ottawa, he didn't just get to meet Martin; he got to spend several weeks with him. Martin brought Flat Mark to work, took him to lunch and to many important meetings. Flat Mark even got the chance to be on hand when Paul Martin was sworn in as Canada's twenty-first prime minister. What's more, Martin's staff took dozens of pictures of Flat Mark during his time on Parliament Hill, and posted them on a website, along with journal entries briefly describing Flat Mark's — and Martin's — busy schedule.

But the most amazing part of Flat Mark's adventure was his trip back to Toronto. Martin didn't mail Mark back to his young creators. On January 20, 2004, Paul Martin, Canada's prime minister, personally returned him to his senders at Fenside Public School.

BOW WOW WOW!!!

The world's smartest dog, Chanda-Leah, was a Toy Poodle from Hamilton, Ontario. With love and coaching from her owner, Sharon Robinson, Chanda learned to do more than 500 tricks on command, earning her star billing in the Guinness world records book as the "dog with the largest repertoire of tricks."

Like many other peppy pooches, Chanda could sit, roll over, shake a paw, fetch a ball and play dead when asked to, but what other cunning canine could skateboard, slam dunk, play piano, add, subtract and multiply? Chanda could. She also used her own little toilet without fail, picked up and put her toys away, brought Robinson a tissue when she sneezed, untied knotted shoelaces, and picked out specific numbers, days of the week and months of the year from cue cards.

Chanda was smart enough to stand at attention when she heard "O Canada." She was also smart enough to know what to do in a no-win situation. When Robinson asks her, "What do you do when you see a big dog?" Chanda laid down and said her prayers.

How Chilly Is It?

Canadian researchers have come up with a new wind chill index. The wind chill index combines both the real air temperature and the effect it has on us. The old index, based on measuring how quickly water froze in different wind conditions in Antarctica, was calculated more than 60 years ago. Now it's based on the amount of heat humans lose from their faces when exposed to cold and wind. The numbers refer to how cold you feel. For instance, if the weather report says it's -10°C outside and the wind chill is -20, you know that when you go outside you'll feel as cold as if it were -20°C on a calm day, with no wind.

American researchers worked on developing the new index too. It's also used in the United States and many other countries around the world.

Really Hot, eh?

Humidex is a Canadian word. It's a scale used to indicate how much warmer you feel on a hot day when there's a lot of moisture, or humidity, in the air. On a really humid day the thermometer might read 30°C, but you might feel as if it's about 5°C warmer than that. Why? Perspiring can't cool your body down as well on a humid day because sweat can't easily evaporate into air that's already got a lot of moisture in it.

. . . that the Sphynx cat originated in Canada? In 1966, a regular hairy house cat living in Toronto gave birth to a hairless kitten named Prune. That kitten, obtained by Siamese cat breeders Ridyah and Yania Bawa, is the ancestor of the rare breed of hairless cat known now as the Sphynx. Early on, the breed was called the "Canadian hairless."

Hey, Dad, how about a trophy?

A new job brought Englishman Frederick Arthur Stanley and his family to Canada in 1888. His seven sons could already skate when they arrived in Ottawa, and it didn't take them long to make friends and learn to play hockey with some local boys who often met at a public rink. When other rink users started complaining that the boys were hogging the ice, the brothers said their dad wouldn't mind if the gang came over to play on a rink in their backyard. Their dad just happened to be Lord Stanley, who had come to Canada to be governor general, and their backyard just happened to be the grounds of Rideau Hall, the governor general's official residence in Ottawa.

The Stanley brothers loved playing hockey, and Arthur, Lord Stanley's third son, became a huge fan of the sport in general. He's the one who came up with the idea of forming an ice hockey association. He and his brother, Algy, also kept bugging their dad to buy a trophy that could be given to each year's amateur hockey champions. Their father finally agreed, and in 1892 announced that he would be donating such a trophy.

Lord Stanley and his family left Canada soon after the silver bowl he bought was first awarded in 1893, but his boys still kept playing hockey back in England. They even formed their own team so they could play just for the fun of it. In 1895, for instance, they challenged a team from Buckingham Palace to a game. George, one of the palace players, would go on to become King George V in 1910. But the "Stanley" brothers weren't intimidated by royalty. They got so many goals against their opponents that it became rather embarrassing to keep score.

The Rideau Rebels hockey team. Lord Stanley's son, Arthur is second from the left in the back row, and his other son Edward is seated far left.

Love That Cup!

When the Montreal Canadiens won the Stanley Cup in 1978, they were honoured with a victory parade. After the parade, one of the team's star players, Guy Lafleur, snatched the famed trophy when no one was looking, jumped into his car and drove west to his home town of Thurso, on the Quebec side of the Ottawa River. Grinning like a little kid, the great Lafleur appeared on his parents' doorstep holding the Stanley Cup. After the excitement in the Lafleur household died down, the star forward took the trophy outside so that more relatives, friends and neighbours could see it and have their picture taken with it. Then he headed back to Montreal and returned the cup to its frantic keepers, who had been looking everywhere for it.

Lafleur was warned never to take Lord Stanley's trophy again without permission. But if Lord Stanley's son, Arthur, had still been alive, he probably would have been pleased to hear that the cup had been in such good, hockey-loving hands.

Snowflakes kept falling on their heads...

. . . but that didn't mean most Albertans felt much like singing about it. After all, there was still a month of summer left when snow started falling on southern and central parts of the province on August 21, 1992. In some places the way-too-early white stuff reached depths of up to 60 centimetres. The snowfall in Edmonton was the earliest ever, according to weather records for that city dating all the way back to 1884.

There's a Long, Long Trail a Winding. . .

When the Trans Canada Trail is completed, you'll be able to hike along it right across Canada, from sea to sea to sea. And if you do, you'll be following the longest recreational path in the world. Officially opened in September 2000, the trail is to be fully connected in time for Canada's 150th birthday in 2017. When it's done, the trail will span more than 24 000 kilometres, passing through more than 1000 communities and through every province and territory.

Cold Cut Puck?

Before rubber hockey pucks were readily available, players in Saskatchewan and Nova Scotia used to saw off slices of tree branches and trunks that were about the right diameter for a puck. Then they'd soak them in water and let them freeze so they'd slide better.

Old boot heels and flattened tin cans also made pretty good puck substitutes.

What's that, eh?

Back in the "good old days" when there were a lot more horses around than there were hockey pucks, kids and adults alike made do with slapping road apples around on roads and frozen ponds. But road apples didn't drop from trees; they dropped from horses. And when the brown lumps of horse manure froze solid, they made great — and free — hockey pucks.

What's that, eh?

In Manitoba and northern Ontario, if you're cutting down on calories you may have given up snacking on jambusters. Calorie counters in Nova Scotia might be avoiding Burlington buns, and weight watchers in Alberta and Saskatchewan could be cutting back on the number of bismarcks they munch for dessert. Jambusters, Burlington buns and bismarks may not be good for you, but they sure do taste good. They're what many of us call jelly- or jam-filled doughnuts.

Here Comes the VERY Young Bride

Marguerite Sedilot, Canada's youngest bride on record, was just eleven years and five months old when she married twenty-year-old Jean Aubuchon of Trois-Rivières in New France (now Quebec) on September 19, 1654. She didn't have any choice in the matter — her father had signed a contract promising she'd marry Aubuchon back in 1643, soon after she was born.

Coffee to go, eh?

The first Tim Horton's was opened in Hamilton, Ontario, in May 1964. Hamilton, with 78 franchises in 2003, now lays claim to being the capital of the "Timbit Nation."

Tim Horton, a National Hockey League defenceman, started the coffee-and-doughnut company with a former police officer, Ron Joyce. When Joyce became sole owner after Horton died in a car crash in 1974, there were 35 shops in the chain. Two years later, the company started selling the still-popular doughnut "holes," or Timbits.

Since then the company has gone on to become a great Canadian success story. By 1995, it had 1000 shops, including several dozen south of the border in the United States. That year, the American burger chain Wendy's bought the business, but left the Canadian firm to run its own show. By 2003, with 2200 franchises, Tim Horton's could brag about bumping McDonald's out of its Number 1 position in Canada.

Apple fritters rule. And don't forget the coffee. And the soup, and the sandwiches, and the iced cappuccino and . . .

Vive l'imagination!

In August 2000, eight-year-old Daniel Helm talked his parents into taking him and his friend, Mark Turner, tubing — riding rapids on inflated rings — on Flatbed Creek, near Tumbler Ridge, British Columbia. At one point Mark fell into the water, so the two boys grabbed their rings and waded ashore. As they stood on the bank, they spotted four indentations in a long, flat section of rock. To the boys, the impressions in the rock formed a pattern that looked like footprints. But if these marks were fossilized footprints, the animal that had made them must have been huge. Daniel and Mark were convinced they were looking at dinosaur tracks!

Daniel's parents figured the boys' imaginations were working overtime, but they let the youngsters take pictures and measurements, and Daniel's dad eventually helped them get in touch with Rich McCrea in Edmonton, an expert on dinosaur footprints. The pictures and measurements Daniel and Mark sent McCrea led to his going with the boys the next summer to check out their find. And what a find it turned out to be!

Daniel and Mark had been right. The footprints, and 22 others that McCrea and his team uncovered, had been made by an ankylosaur, or armoured dinosaur, millions of years ago. What's more, while examining the footprints, McCrea discovered some dinosaur bones nearby. Suddenly everyone could envision what Daniel and Mark had imagined a year earlier — a huge, four-limbed reptile lumbering down to Flatbed Creek for a drink.

Towering T. Rex

Drumheller, Alberta, about 140 kilometres northeast of Calgary, is said to be the dinosaur capital of the world. It is located in a region of the province known as the Badlands, where some of the greatest dinosaur fossils ever discovered have been found. It's home to the world-famous Royal Tyrrell Museum, where amazing dinosaur skeletons are displayed. It's also home to the world's largest dinosaur monument. The steel, foam and fibreglass model of a *Tyrannosaurus rex* towers 26.2 metres over Drumheller, its tooth-filled mouth gaping open as if it's about to roar. A stairway inside the monster leads visitors to an observation platform in the giant's massive jaws.

DID YOU KNOW...

. . . that the Northwest Territories is the only place in North America that doesn't have rectangular-shaped licence plates? The NWT plate is in the shape of a polar bear. And did you know that *nanuk* is the Inuktitut word for polar bear?

What's that, eh?

Muskeg is a Canadian word that comes from the Cree word *maskeq*, meaning swamp or bog. It's a spongy buildup of moss, leaves and other decaying plant material. Water lies very close to its surface. Muskeg covers most of the Hudson Bay Lowlands, and many other parts of northern Canada.

Hands Off Comet's Record

On August 5, 2002, Canadian Tom Comet set a new world juggling record. He performed his death-defying stunt before hundreds of screaming fans at a daredevil stage show in Edinburgh, Scotland. Even in his expert hands, Comet's feat is incredibly dangerous, so DON'T EVEN THINK ABOUT IMITATING HIM. What he did was throw and catch three 5.5-kilogram roaring, whirling chainsaws 44 times. During his record-breaking effort, he stunned the crowd when he dropped one saw after just 22 throws, 20 throws short of the existing record. But the cool Comet picked it up and started all over again. Forty-four throws later he was champion of the chainsaw juggling world. Triumphant, he raised his scarred arms in victory.

What's that, eh?

During the Depression of the early 1930s, many Canadians were out of work. Some people who could no longer afford gasoline used their cars like wagons, hitching them to horses or oxen. These contraptions were sarcastically referred to as Bennett buggies, named after Richard Bedford (R.B.) Bennett, Canada's unpopular prime minister from 1930 to 1935. Many people blamed him for much of the hardship they had to put up with when his Conservatives were in power.

*On average, lightning strikes kill 6 to 10 Canadians and seriously injure 60 to 70 each year.
* Lightning also starts about 4000 forest fires annually.
* Generally speaking, most Canadians are more frightened of lightning than they are of another dangerous element of weather, but you should know that exposure to cold kills at least 80 people in Canada annually.
* On average, lightning lights up Vancouver skies just six times a year.
* The number of flashes for other cities includes: Quebec City, 51; Ottawa, 90; and Toronto, 200. Windsor, Ontario, tops the list with 251.

Queen
of the Skies

Amelia Earhart, the world's most famous female aviator, vowed to learn to fly one day when she was in Canada. Earhart, an American, came to Toronto in 1917 after graduating from high school. There she served as a volunteer nurse at a military hospital, caring for wounded World War I soldiers. Several air force squadrons trained in Toronto and there was a lot of air traffic above the city at the time. Earhart was fascinated by the planes and spent much of her spare time at an airport in the north end of Toronto watching pilots-in-training practise takeoffs and landings. Her love of flying took root there, as did her determination to become a pilot. She returned to the United States in 1919 and went up in a plane for the first time in 1920. A year later she kept the promise she had made to herself in Toronto, completing her flying lessons as quickly as she could manage to get instruction and flying time.

In 1932, a year after Charles Lindbergh became the first person to fly solo across the Atlantic, Earhart became the first woman to do so. Three years later, she became the first person to make a solo flight from Hawaii to California. In 1937, she took off with a navigator to fly all the way around the world. After completing two-thirds of that incredible journey, she, her navigator and the plane disappeared somewhere over the Pacific Ocean.

Brave Hunters of the North

In 2003, the folks of South River, Ontario, held the first annual blackfly hunt, claiming it would greatly reduce the number of the nasty little biters in the area. If only . . .

The month-long hunting season opened on May 3, with town officials giving enthusiastic kickoff speeches and children taking turns whacking a blackfly-shaped piñata. When the candies finally spilled out of the decapitated blackfly, the hunt was on.

This was one very well-organized event. Hunters had to get a licence to be eligible for the prizes that would be awarded at the official weigh-in on June 7. Hunters were told that they should release flies under 2.5 millimetres whenever possible. They were warned that anyone caught injecting individual flies with water to increase their weight would be disqualified. So would anyone caught adding other species such as mosquitoes to their catch. Anyone caught breaking hunt rules could be used as blackfly bait. Using trained hunting frogs was allowed . . . as long as owners kept them on a leash. Spreading jam and dabbing perfume behind the ears to attract flies was also permitted.

On June 7, prizes were handed out to the most successful hunters, to the best dressed hunters and to the authors of the best limericks or short poems about blackflies.

The event was such a success that on June 9, top hunter Rusty Perkins was interviewed on CBC Radio's "As It Happens" to talk about his winning techniques.

Give South Riverites a round of applause. They scored 10 out of 10 on the "great Canadian sense of humour" scale.

Famous Family

A Nova Scotian named Rose Fortune may very well have been the world's first policewoman. Fortune's family escaped from slavery in Virginia in 1783 and settled in Annapolis Royal when she was 10. When she grew up, Fortune simply put herself in charge of policing the community. To keep ruffians in line after dark, the tiny woman established curfews and went around town sending home anyone still out and about after her deadline. Fortune died in 1864. Seven generations later, in 1984, one of her descendants, Duarene E. Lewis, was elected mayor of Annapolis Royal. She was Nova Scotia's first black mayor.

Helllllllllllllllllllllllp!

Winnipeg was the first city in the world to come up with the system of dialing 9-1-1 to get help in an emergency.

RRRRRING

The world's first long-distance phone call was made in Canada on August 10, 1876. Alexander Graham Bell placed that call from his family's home near Brantford to an assistant in Paris, Ontario, (not Paris, France) about 15 kilometres away.

RRRRRING

RRRRRING

The first long-distance call made on the Prairies was one placed between Edmonton, Alberta and Battleford, Saskatchewan in November 1887.

The Ultimate Lawyer's Joke

When wealthy Toronto lawyer Charles Vance Millar died in 1926, his will showed him to be quite the jokester. Millar had been a bachelor, so he didn't have to worry about leaving his estate to his children. Instead, he drew up a will that would test his belief that everyone can be tempted to give in to greed, if the price is right.

With a delicious sense of mischief, Millar included items in his will that he knew would cause trouble. For instance, he left shared use of a luxurious house to three lawyers who couldn't stand being with each other. He also left valuable shares in the Ontario Jockey Club to two people who had spoken out for years against the evils of racetrack gambling. He even left shares in a brewery to anti-drinking ministers.

But what made Millar's will famous was his leaving most of his wealth to the Toronto woman who had the most children in the 10 years after he died. The media went wild over this bequest, dubbing the race to have babies The Great Stork Derby.

When Millar died, he had no idea that the Great Depression would hit people so hard a few years later, or that his estate — from shares in the building of the tunnel between Windsor, Ontario, and Detroit, Michigan — would eventually be worth three-quarters of a million dollars. But by the 1930s, many poor mothers in Toronto were dreaming of winning that prize.

Questions about whether stillborn or out-of-wedlock babies should count took years to settle in court, but finally four women who had each had nine children by 1936 were declared the winners. So the Stork Derby ended in a four-way tie, with each woman getting $125 000 — a very large fortune back in the Dirty Thirties.

Just the Stats

*In 2002, after a rainy June and a hot, humid early July — ideal breeding conditions for mosquitoes — Winnipeggers had to put up with more than 25 bites per minute when the bloodsuckers came out to feed each evening.

*But that doesn't come close to the city's all-time record in the summer of 1991: 184 bites per minute. Don't scratch.

... that one of the most effective bug repellents in the world is a Canadian concoction? Charlie Coll of Truro, Nova Scotia, created Muskol in the 1970s. Shering-Plough Canada, a big drug company in Mississauga, Ontario, bought Coll's business in 1982, but Charlie wasn't forgotten. He's the man pictured on bottles of Muskol.

The Grizzly Man

In 1984, 20-year-old Troy James Hurtubise of North Bay, Ontario, survived a grizzly bear attack while visiting British Columbia. Three years later, after watching the film *Robocop*, Hurtubise got one wild and wacky idea. He would build himself a protective suit that would let him get close enough to learn more about the type of bear that had attacked him.

Each suit Hurtubise built was an improvement over the previous one, but some of his testing methods were pretty dramatic. Once he threw himself 45 metres down the Niagara Escarpment to see how well his suit withstood such a bumpy tumble. A few other times, he faced a 3-tonne truck going 40 kilometres an hour head-on, and he also let it run over him more than a dozen times. Fortunately, his armour always held out, but just barely sometimes. However, the stronger he made his suit, the harder it was for him to get around in it.

Hurtubise's sixth effort, the Ursus Mark VI, was a massive outfit made of titanium, chain mail, heavy plastic and lots of duct tape. It weighed nearly 65 kilograms and cost him a fortune to build. It's the suit featured in *Project Grizzly*, a Canadian film made in 1996 documenting his elaborate testing and his trip back to B.C. to get up close and personal with a grizzly. The film shows Hurtubise suited up in the Ursus Mark VI as he's battered by a swinging log, bashed by burly bikers with baseball bats, hit with a shotgun blast and struck by flying arrows. The suit kept him safe, but he could barely move in it. When he and a team of friends finally got to B.C., they spent days searching for bears, but didn't come across one until they were about to leave. By then it was too late for Hurtubise to run back to the suit and put it on before the grizzly took off.

This misadventure left Hurtubise deeply in debt. Creditors eventually confiscated the Ursus Mark VI and he lost his scrap metal business. What's more, his labour of love was ridiculed when *Project Grizzly* came out in 1999. But Hurtubise didn't give up. At last report, he was working on the Ursus Mark VII, a suit supposedly even stronger. But all he really wants to do with it is study, close up, the type of bear that attacked him when he was young. He definitely deserves an A for effort.

You Don't Say

Did you know that one of the sons of Charles Dickens, the famous nineteenth-century English author, was an original member of the North West Mounted Police?

Francis Jeffrey Dickens was the fifth of Charles's ten children. In 1874, thanks to a family friend — Canada's governor general, Lord Dufferin — Dickens was named a sub-inspector in the newly formed police force that would become the Royal Canadian Mounted Police. He was posted to many trouble spots in western Canada and served in the force until resigning in 1886. Some accounts suggest that he wasn't all the force expected of its officers, but his dad was famous, so two scarlet-coated Mounties were on hand in September 2002 for the ceremonial unveiling of a new headstone on the grave of Inspector Francis J. Dickens in Moline, Illinois. Dickens died there of a heart attack at age 42.

Jeffrey Dickens is second from the left in the back row.

One Rock at a Time

About 20 kilometres west of Kindersley, Saskatchewan, a strange stone wall cuts across the fields. It's a big wall. Taller than an adult at its low points, it reaches heights of 5 metres in some places, and stretches on for at least a kilometre. But the wall doesn't "do" anything. It doesn't fence anything in or keep anyone out. It doesn't surround a special building or mark off a famous battle site. It's just there.

Farmer Albert Johnson didn't start out to build a wall when he moved the first rocks into place back in 1962. He just wanted to tidy up a pile of stones that he had cleared from part of his property. So he lined them up, one by one. Then he began stacking them carefully on top of each other.

For 40 years Johnson collected, sorted and piled up stones, creating the massive dry-stone (mortar-free) wall. Day after day, week after week, month after month he worked on it, without really knowing why. He just felt he had to.

Now the wall sits there, doing nothing in particular except give people something to talk about and to remember "Stonewall" Johnson by.

Where did you say?

Head-Smashed-In Buffalo Jump in southwestern Alberta tops most lists of favourite Canadian place names. The last part of the name recalls how, for nearly 6000 years, the Plains First Nations people hunted buffalo by chasing them over steep cliffs there. The trails leading to the cliffs and the thousands of skeletons in the area are some of the best evidence of how aboriginal people lived so long ago. But, according to a Blackfoot and Peguis legend, the "Head-Smashed-In" part doesn't refer to what happened to the buffalos' heads. The legend tells of how a young man stood under a ledge below the cliff so he could have a better view of the hunt. That wasn't such a good idea. His skull was crushed by the buffalo crashing to the ground around him.

In 1981, the United Nations designated the place a World Heritage site.

Starstruck

A Canadian, Gladys Louise Smith, was one of the founders of United Artists, the famous movie studio. Smith was born in Toronto in 1892. When she became a popular stage actress in New York, she changed her name to Mary Pickford. Pickford went on to become a great film star. In 1919, she and her actor husband, Douglas Fairbanks, together with two other film giants, Charlie Chaplin and D. W. Griffith, formed United Artists — now one of the most successful film companies in the world.

Another famous film company also has a Canadian connection. Eliezer Meir (later called Louis B. Mayer) was born in Russia in 1885. He and his family emigrated to Canada when he was a boy. He grew up in Saint John, New Brunswick, but moved to the United States when he was a young man. There he would go from scrap metal dealer to theatre owner to owner of a chain of theatres and, in 1917, to founder of his own filmmaking company. That company eventually merged with two others. If you haven't already guessed, he's the "Mayer" in Metro-Goldwyn-Mayer (MGM).

In 2004 Pickford and Mayer were both given stars on Canada's Walk of Fame in downtown Toronto.

D'oh!

On May 30, 2003, Winnipeg's city council awarded an honorary citizenship to their most famous native son — TV star Homer Simpson. Homer was on hand for the ceremony, as were officials from Global Television, the network that carries "The Simpsons" in Canada.

American cartoonist Matt Groening once joked that because he had based his Homer creation on his own Canadian-born father, Homer Simpson must be Canadian.

When asked where his father had been born, he tossed out the first Prairie city that came to mind — Winnipeg.

It turns out that Homer Groening was actually born in the Saskatchewan hamlet of Main Centre. But that fact of life wasn't about to stop Winnipeg from giving the fictional Homer the keys to the city. Having him as a native son was a claim to fame that city councillors couldn't resist.

You want big?
You'll get BIG.

When FedEx came looking for a big box to use in a 2002 Super Bowl promotion, folks at Norampac Inc. in Toronto decided they might as well aim for a world record while they were at it. Sure enough, the huge corrugated cardboard box they assembled in downtown Toronto on October 15, 2001, was a record breaker. Made under a large tent to keep out the rain (the box would have collapsed if it had got wet), the finished box measured a whopping 9.34 x 3.04 x 2.19 metres, big enough to hold a school bus.

Huggable High

On April 23, 2004, students, staff, parents and other friends of St. Matthew's Catholic High School in Orleans, Ontario — 5117 bodies in all — gathered outside the building. Crowding together in a huge circle, they all reached out and hugged one another. After 10 seconds they broke apart, cheering. They had just set a record — for the largest group hug in the world.

He said What?

"When you're a short actor you stand on apple boxes, you walk on a ramp. When you're a short star everybody else walks in a ditch."
— Michael J. Fox

Fox, the star of many TV series and films, was born in Edmonton, Alberta. He is 162 centimetres (5'4") tall.

The Fastest Ice in the World

That's the claim to fame of the covered speed-skating oval built for the Winter Olympics held in Calgary, Alberta, in 1988.

The ice on the 400-metre-long track is carefully maintained to make sure that world champion skaters zipping around it have the smoothest, hardest ice on which to achieve record-breaking speeds. The temperature, humidity and air flow inside the building are also carefully controlled to ensure that the exceptionally high quality of the ice remains the same during competitions watched by thousands of heat- and moisture-generating fans.

So from 1988 until 2002, when the Winter Olympics were held in Salt Lake City, Utah (USA), most world speed-skating records were broken at Calgary's Olympic Oval. Then, for a few years, the track in Salt Lake City claimed to have the fastest ice, and rightly so. But as of March 2007, Salt Lake was the site of just 10 record-breaking skates, whereas 12 current world records were set in Calgary, making it once again home to the fastest ice in the world.

Riding High in Thunder Bay

On July 1, 2003, Thunder Bay, Ontario, resident Brad Graham rode his bicycle around the parking lot of Thunder Bay's community auditorium and into the *Guinness World Records* book. He didn't ride very far and he didn't ride very fast, but he did ride very high above the ground. Graham's homemade SkyCycle was a wonderfully wacky creation that measured 4.34 metres from the top of its handlebars to the bottom of its two standard bike wheels, setting a record for the world's tallest rideable bicycle.

GUINNESS
WORLD RECORDS™

CERTIFICATE

Brad Graham (Canada)
successfully rode his SkyCycle,
which measures 4.34 m (14 ft 3 in)
to the handlebars,
on 1 July 2003
at Thunder Bay, Ontario, Canada.
The bicycle has only two wheels
and no stabilisers of any kind
Keeper of the Records
GUINNESS WORLD RECORDS LTD

Riding Higher
in Winnipeg

Not to be outdone, on June 26, 2004, Terry Goertzen, a Mennonite church pastor in Winnipeg, Manitoba, rode even higher. Like Brad Graham, Goertzen loved building zany bikes, and the one that he rode 300 metres to qualify for the World's Tallest Bike record was 5.5 metres high. Goertzen's bicycle was similar to Graham's, with the main frame forming a ladder up to the seat. The chain that drove the wheels was 11 metres long!

How short Is It?

When a crop is especially poor, some folks in Saskatchewan say:

"This year the crop's so short that the gophers have to kneel to eat."

That's short!

DID YOU KNOW...

...that the first woman to fly a plane in Newfoundland was the great American aviator Amelia Earhart?

In 1928, when Earhart became the first woman to cross the Atlantic by plane, she and two other pilots, William Stultz and Lew Cordon, took off from Trepassey, Newfoundland. And four years later, on May 20, 1932, when she set out on her historic solo flight across the Atlantic Ocean — becoming the third person and the first woman to do so — she again took off in Newfoundland, this time from Harbour Grace. On board she carried a Thermos of hot soup made by a local resident, Rose Archibald.

Round and Round She Goes

Wendy Killoran, a mother and schoolteacher from London, Ontario, also chose Newfoundland as the starting point of a challenging journey. It was also where she ended it.

A keen kayaker since 1991, Killoran set out from Isle Aux Morts, Newfoundland, on May 5, 2006. One hundred and four days later, after kayaking 2700 kilometres, she paddled back to shore at Isle Aux Morts, becoming the first woman to circumnavigate, or go all the way around, Newfoundland.

A year earlier, Killoran also became the first woman to kayak around an entire province — Prince Edward Island — and in 2004, she paddled around the world's largest freshwater island — Manitoulin Island in Lake Huron.

What's in a Name?

Plenty, if you're Cecil Nesmo, a rancher near
Manyberries, a small town in the badlands of southern
Alberta. For nearly 60 years, researchers had been
visiting the Nesmo family's property looking for — and
finding — fossils. After all, this was dinosaur country,
and Nesmo never turned away a genuine dinosaur
hunter. That's why, in 2001, he was more than willing
to let Michael Ryan, a graduate student of paleontology
(prehistoric life) from the University of Calgary, camp
out on his property to examine some very old exposed
bones. Those bones would turn out to be part of the
skeleton of a type of dinosaur no one had ever seen
before.

Tests would later reveal that the "new" dinosaur was
very old — about 78 million years old — and that it was
a member of the ceratops family. But as well as having
the huge horns of dinosaurs like triceratops, the skull
also had a large spiked collar, or frill, a lot like those
found on another group of ceratops called centrosaurs.
The combination of these two features had never
before been found on one dinosaur.

It took Ryan a few years to finish studying his exciting
discovery of a new kind of dinosaur, but when he proudly
published the news of his find in a scientific journal,

he also announced to the world the name he had given it — *Albertaceratops nesmoi*. When Cecil Nesmo heard the news, he was surprised and honoured. He had never dreamed when he let Ryan camp out on his ranch that one day he would have a dinosaur named after him.

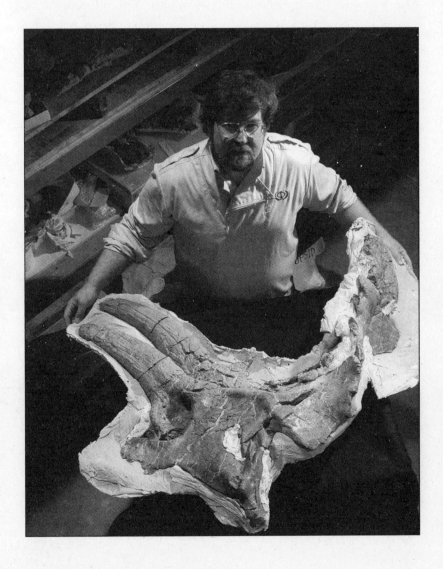

One Land, Many Voices

Canada has two official languages, English and French. Our provinces and territories, however, are all over the map. Quebec has one official language: French. New Brunswick is the only province with two official languages: English and French. The other provinces have not made any languages official, nor has Yukon Territory, but the territory of Nunavut has three official languages: English, French and Inuktitut.

And the Northwest Territories? Beneath the snowflake-inspired crown atop the mace, or ceremonial rod, that symbolizes the government's authority are the words "One land, many voices" — showing how committed the government is to respecting *all* the languages used by its people. So the Northwest Territories has 11 official languages: English, French, Chipewyan, Cree, Gwich'in, Inuktitut, Inuinnaqtun, Inuvialuktun, North Slavey, South Slavey and Dogrib.

DID YOU KNOW...

. . . that documents in the national library in Beijing, China, support claims by some experts that Chinese Buddhist monks visited what's now British Columbia hundreds of years before European explorers arrived there? The writings of a monk named Hoei Shin describe his incredible voyages of exploration, including references to stopping along what might have been the B.C. coast way back in 449.

It's a Blockbuster!

When the Canadian National Exhibition (also known as the CNE or the Ex) opened on Friday, August 17, 2007, in Toronto, Ontario, visitors were invited to join in the fun of building the world's tallest tower — out of Lego blocks!

Over a period of three days, thousands of kids and adults snapped together hundreds of thousands of the small plastic bricks. Guided by engineers from Lego's headquarters in Denmark, they built separate sections that were lifted by workers in the bucket of a large crane and carefully placed securely on top of each other. By Monday the multi-coloured tower was tall enough to make its mark on Toronto's skyline, but no one could say for sure just how tall it was. Strong winds made it too dangerous for the crane to hoist someone up to the top with a tape measure.

Finally, on Wednesday, the measurement was made and it was official — the tower was a record-breaker. At 29.03 metres — about nine storeys tall — the giant four-sided structure was 0.45 metres higher than the previous record holder, a tower built in Carlsbad, California, a few months earlier.

With up to 100 raccoons per square kilometre, Toronto, Ontario, is known as the raccoon capital of North America and maybe even of the world. In rural areas of the province, where you might expect to find more of the masked critters hanging out, the population is just 4 to 12 raccoons per square kilometre.

What's that, eh?

Tarabish, anyone? What is it? It's a card game, often called tarbish, or 'bish, on Cape Breton Island, in Nova Scotia. This is the only place in the whole world where lots of people know how to play the game and absolutely love it. In fact, on March 3, 2007, hundreds of them registered in two-person teams for the 19th annual World Tarabish Championship tournament at the Nova Scotia Community College in Sydney.

He Nailed It!

Allan B. Dove, a chemical engineer who started working for The Steel Company of Canada (Stelco) in Hamilton, Ontario, in the early 1930s, was really interested in nails. Old and new, tiny tacks and big spikes, square-cut and round, he collected them all and studied them carefully, and after years of research, he came up with an idea for a new and improved style of nail.

Dove figured out that a spiral-shaped nail would twist, rather than pound, its way into wood, making hammering it in easier. It would also be less likely to split the wood and would grip it much better than a smooth, round nail. His colleagues at Stelco loved the idea and patented Dove's invention — the ardox nail — in 1954. Ardox nails are now used around the world, and builders have a Canadian to thank.

Just the Stats

On average, Canadians gobble up more than 14 kilograms of bananas every year. Probably some are being eaten on the way to work. Apparently, nearly 40 per cent of Canadians between the ages of 18 and 27 eat breakfast on the run.

Big Time in B.C.

It's 1100 metres above sea level. Its main street looks as though it belongs to a town in the German Alps. German food is on the menu of many of its cafés and restaurants. One of those restaurants is in a 350-year-old Bavarian building — but the building isn't in Bavaria. It was taken apart there and shipped in pieces all the way to British Columbia where it was carefully reassembled in Kimberley, known since the 1970s as "the Bavarian city of the Rockies."

Kimberley B.C.

Introducing a German alpine theme to Kimberley was intended to attract more tourists, and the plan worked. Visitors strolling along the *Platzl* — the German word for the pedestrian mall there — are delighted when Happy Hans pops out of his house to greet them. Hans, who's just 1.2 metres tall, is Kimberley's lederhosen-wearing mascot. Every hour on the hour he steps out on his balcony to yodel for anyone who'll listen. His house is a tourist draw too. Nearly 7 metres high, it's the largest working cuckoo clock in North America, and one of the largest in the world. Hans, rather than a cuckoo bird, pops out of it. And if someone wants to see and hear him between scheduled appearances, he's very accommodating. A few coins slipped into a slot are all it takes for him to give a command performance.

Local Flavour

Kimberley's residents have every reason to be proud
of their really big cuckoo clock, but the popular German
sausages cooked up for visitors there lose out in the
bragging department to the Ukrainian sausage in Mundare,
Alberta. The 700 or so folks living in this small town
east of Edmonton are so proud of the garlic-flavoured,
prize-winning kielbasa made at Stawnichy's, the local meat
processing plant, that they've erected a monument to it —
a 12.8-metre-high fibreglass sausage coil weighing six tons.
It's the largest kielbasa in the world!

DID YOU KNOW...

...that on December 7, 1898, Canada
issued the world's first Christmas stamp? It was
a two-cent stamp bearing a picture of a map of
the world, with "XMAS 1898" printed across the
bottom of the map. And nearly 100 years later,
Canada Post issued the world's first "do-it-yourself"
stamps, with a blank space on which you could attach
special occasion stickers or draw your own decorations.

Riding the River

According to a small but keen group of Montrealers, you don't need to live near an ocean coastline to be able to catch a big wave on a regular basis. You just have to tuck your surfboard under your arm, stroll down to an area behind the housing complex known as Habitat '67, and slip into the swirling waters of the mighty St. Lawrence River near the city's port. It's there you'll find a 30-metre-wide standing, or stationary, wave that surfers love to ride, no matter how cold the water might be.

Look at Me!

Charles Connell, a lumberman born in Carleton County, New Brunswick, in 1810, was a popular politician in that province both before and after Confederation. A strong believer in responsible government, he worked hard on behalf of his constituents right up until his death in 1873. But in 1860 he made a foolish move that left voters wondering, "Charles, what were you thinking?"

In 1859 New Brunswick's lieutenant-governor appointed him postmaster general and asked him to organize the design and production of new 1-, 5-, 10- and 12½-cent stamps. The new stamps were supposed to go on sale on May 1, 1860. But when the lieutenant-governor was sent a set for approval in late April, he was stunned. The 5-cent stamp was unacceptable. He had expected to see a portrait of Queen Victoria on it, but that picture had been replaced with one of a man he knew well — none other than Charles Connell himself!

Connell was ordered not to release the stamp on May 1st and to get replacements printed as quickly as possible. He did as he was told, and then quickly resigned as postmaster general. He personally bought all 500 000 copies of the rejected stamps and burned almost all of them, saving just a few sheets as souvenirs for his daughters and a close friend. Supposedly, his daughters destroyed theirs, not wanting to keep evidence of their father's foolishness, and voters eventually forgave and forgot, electing him as a member of Canada's new Parliament in 1867. But we still don't have the answer to the question they puzzled over in 1860 — "Charles, what were you thinking?"

Chinook Can't Lose

Back in the 1990s a Canadian-made computer program named Chinook beat the world's best checkers players. But Chinook's creator, Jonathan Schaeffer — a computer science professor at the University of Alberta — wasn't satisfied with having his software earn the checkers champ title. He wanted to make sure that any challengers — human or computer — might be able to come up with a draw against Chinook, but they could never win.

Schaeffer began working on Chinook in 1989. Eighteen years later, in July 2007, after millions of calculations using dozens of computers, he and his team of U of A researchers announced that they had finally achieved that goal: their new and improved version of Chinook can never be beaten.

Why did it take so long to perfect Chinook? After all, checkers seems like a pretty simple game when compared to chess, for example. But there are 500 billion billion possible moves in a checker game! By comparison, there are just 765 possible moves in tic-tac-toe.

…that the first Scouts' Apple Day in Canada was held in Saint John, New Brunswick, on January 30, 1932? Eli Boyaner, a local optometrist, came up with the idea of having the Boy Scouts — no girls were allowed back then — hand out apples in exchange for whatever donations people wanted to make to support local scouting activities.

The popular fundraiser now takes place each October when fresh, crisp apples are more readily available and when the weather is usually much nicer than in January. But on that first Apple Day, young Scouts didn't let stinging sleet and pelting rain stop them from handing out about 21 000 apples.

The Great Big Escape

First Shu Mei of Newmarket, Ontario, smelled it when she opened her door one morning in mid-July, 2007. Then she saw it — a huge patty of poop way too big to scoop — on her front lawn. Shu Mei stayed clear of the reeking pile, but she did take a closer look at some of her flowers and a tree in her yard. Clearly, something had been eating them — something big.

205

Shortly before Shu Mei made her smelly discovery, the 9-1-1 calls had started coming in, but at first dispatchers had trouble believing what they were hearing. People were reporting seeing elephants strolling down the street.

The reports were accurate. The cord feeding an electrified fence around a visiting circus's elephant enclosure had been accidentally unplugged, and two of the three large beasts — Bunny and Susie — had decided to check out the neighbourhood. Susie didn't go far, but Bunny made it to Shu Mei's street and stopped to snack on her plants and fertilize her lawn. Fortunately for all concerned, Bunny and Susie were gentle giants, and their trainers had no problem shepherding them back to the circus grounds. One of the trainers even came back and scooped up the poop from Shu Mei's lawn.

Another Critter on the Lam

In July 1990, a pig that was determined not to become bacon escaped from a slaughterhouse in Red Deer, Alberta. Francis, as someone named him, managed to roam free much longer than Bunny and Susie, the elephants who went walkabout in Newmarket. In fact Francis was on the lam for nearly five months, foraging for food in parks and avoiding several attempts to capture him. The longer he roamed free, the more famous he became, and the more people supported him as if he were the underdog in a sports event.

When he was finally cornered he had earned the affection of so many Red Deer residents that no one dared send him back to the abattoir. As the plaque beside a large statue erected in his honour recounts, "This freedom-loving pig was finally captured and spent his remaining life on a local farm."

Runaway Balloon

Elephants and pigs on the loose in a Canadian city are newsworthy, but a helium-filled balloon on the run? What's so unusual about that? Don't helium balloons escape every day and drift up, up and away? True, but they aren't huge — 25 storeys high — and they're not carrying a gondola loaded with more than half a million dollars worth of scientific instruments. That one got away on August 24, 1998.

The balloon was the centrepiece of a joint research project involving the Canadian Space Agency, Environment Canada and scientists from several universities and a few private companies. The project was designed to gather important information on the thinning of the stratosphere's ozone layer. The idea was to launch the gigantic balloon from an old air base at Vanscoy, Saskatchewan, on a calm, clear day, letting it float 35 kilometres up through the ozone layer, collecting and sending data back to Earth as it rose. And the balloon did exactly that.

It was launched in the early hours of August 24th, drifted straight up and remained overhead until late in the day when researchers sent it a signal that was supposed to release the gondola and let it parachute gently back to the ground. But the gondola didn't detach. Then the wind came up and the balloon drifted away, heading east over Manitoba and Ontario, toward the St. Lawrence River and into airspace used by commercial flights.

Air traffic controllers were informed of its presence and warned pilots to avoid it. On it sailed, over Quebec and the Maritimes, until two Canadian fighter jets were sent to shoot it down near Newfoundland. But despite being riddled with bullet holes, the balloon kept going. American and British fighter planes targeted it too, but they couldn't stop it. Radio and television networks tracked its journey as if it were Santa's sleigh making deliveries on Christmas Eve.

Eventually the balloon entered Russian airspace and, finally, to the relief of everyone involved in the project, on September 2, 1998, it came down in a field on Mariehamn Island, Finland, in the Baltic Sea. Two Finnish weather scientists located it, packed up the gondola's valuable instruments, and shipped them back to Canada by plane, not balloon. Researchers in Canada were delighted to find that the instruments were still working despite the bullet dents. The project had been much more exciting than they had expected, but it had worked, at least from a data-collection point of view.

. . . that the slowest growing tree discovered in the world is clinging to a cliff of the Niagara escarpment in Ontario? In 1996, the tiny, twisted 155-year-old white cedar was just 10.2 centimetres high and weighed a minuscule 17 grams. And if the age of some of its dead relatives is any indication of what lies ahead, it's still got a lot of living — if not a lot of growing — to do. Scientists discovered one dead tree that had reached the incredible age of 1653 years!

IT'S A SHOVEL!
IT'S A SHIELD!
IT'S A FLOP

When Sam Hughes's personal secretary, Ena MacAdam, came back from a trip to Switzerland in 1913, she told her boss about a shovel she had seen there that might come in handy for soldiers fighting in the trenches in Europe during World War I. Hughes, after making a few changes in the design, got a patent for the shovel in her name, and ordered nearly 25 000 of them from a steel company in Pennsylvania. Then he shipped at least 22 000 across to Britain to be given to Canadian troops.

The MacAdam shovel, also known as the Hughes shovel, was a short-handled one with a hole in the middle of the blade. Soldiers were supposed to use the shovel as a shield while aiming their rifles through the hole. But Brigadier General McRae was not impressed with the newest piece of equipment to arrive from Canada. He pointed out to his superiors that the hole made it less efficient as a digging tool, and the steel blade and iron handle weighed about 2.3 kilograms, an extra weight that already loaded-down soldiers didn't need to bear. Besides, the blade wasn't thick enough to stop all bullets and was barely big enough to shield the head. McRae recommended that the 50 tonnes of metal he'd been shipped in the shape of shovels be melted down and put to far better use in fighting the war.

They said What?

"The aeroplane is an invention of the devil and will never play any part in such a serious business as the defence of a nation."

— Samuel Hughes, 1914

Sam Hughes was the equivalent of today's minister of defence for Canada from 1911 to 1916, and in many historians' opinions, did a terrible job.

". . . a conceited lunatic."
— Prince Arthur, Duke of Connaught, 1914, referring to Sam Hughes

Prince Arthur, one of Queen Victoria's sons, was Canada's governor general from 1911 to 1916, at the same time as Sam Hughes was the minister in charge of Canada's military.

Just the Stats

Around 1850 as many as 100 million bison, or buffalo, roamed the Canadian prairies. By about 1880, after just 30 years of overhunting and settlers moving west, there were only a few hundred left.

DID YOU KNOW...

...that Hairy Hill, Alberta, is named after itchy buffalo?

Hairy Hill is a small town in northeastern Alberta that started out as a post office and trading post in the 1900s. When settlers first arrived there, some buffalo were still roaming freely in Two Hills County. When these large beasts wanted to get rid of biting insects burrowing into their furry hides, they'd rub up against the many clumps of prickly bushes covering the hillside, leaving the branches covered with strands of brown hair. Until people actually saw the buffalo using the plants as back-scratchers, they weren't sure what to make of the strange-looking shrubs. But one thing they were sure of was that the hill was pretty hairy and they referred to it that way. The name, like the hair, stuck.

As for Brownie Bay and Fudge Lake in Manitoba, no one seems to know how these places got stuck with such sweet names.

A Rookie's Nightmare

In 1985–86 rookie defenceman Steve Smith was thrilled to be playing with the NHL's Edmonton Oilers, a team that included such hockey greats as Paul Coffey and Wayne Gretzky. The Oilers had had a fantastic regular season, and appeared to be heading for their third Stanley Cup championship in a row. But they still had to get past another Alberta team, the Calgary Flames, to make it to the finals.

The best-of-seven series with the Flames was tied 3-3 when the two teams met in Edmonton on April 30, 1986, to play the tiebreaker. The score was tied 2-2 in the third period of the must-win game when Smith tried to clear the puck out of his end. But to his horror he passed the puck across his own net where it hit the stick of Grant Fuhr, the Oilers' goaltender, and bounced into the net.

The game ended 3-2 for the Flames — who went on to lose the final series to the Montreal Canadiens. And although the closest Flames player to the play was credited with the goal, Smith, the other Oilers and the Edmonton fans knew that it was one of their own who had accidentally scored the winning goal — for the wrong team! It was a goal Smith always wanted to forget.

Where's an Invisibility Cloak When You Need One?

During a 1968 NHL hockey game between the Boston Bruins and the St. Louis Blues, it was a player, and not a puck, that went astray, leaving the Blues' Noel Picard — another defenceman — open to friendly razzing for years to come. When Picard's shift on the ice ended, he headed for the open door in the boards and slid onto the bench for a well-earned rest. Then he looked around and saw that he was surrounded by opponents, not teammates. Picard had joined the Bruins' bench.

Stung by the fans' laughter and facing the furious glare of his coach, Picard slipped over the boards and raced to the Blues' bench, but not before the referee saw what he was doing and added to Picard's misery by blowing the whistle and penalizing St. Louis — for having too many men on the ice!

...that the small town of Viking, Alberta, is home to one of the most famous families in National Hockey League history? Six of the sons of Grace and Louis Sutter of Viking became NHL players, and when their playing days were over, four of them also went on to become NHL coaches and managers.

To honour the young men who put Viking on the map, the town's arena was decorated with a large mural featuring the talented brothers — Brian, Duane, Rich, Darryl, Brent and Ron Sutter.

Just the Stats

Altogether, the Sutter brothers played more than 5000 games in the National Hockey League. And on a per capita basis, the arena in Viking has produced more players who made it to the NHL than any other arena in the world.

Free Food to the Rescue

Built and launched in Liverpool, England, in 1864, the SS *Moravian* safely shuttled passengers and cargo across the Atlantic Ocean for several years. The large, sturdy ship did have one close call sailing from Ireland to Quebec in September 1875, when it rammed into an iceberg. Fortunately, it escaped with just minor damage to its hull and continued on its way.

But on December 30, 1881, as it sailed east from
Portland, Maine, in stormy weather, the *Moravian's* luck
ran out off Cape Sable, the southern tip of Nova Scotia.
The treacherous waters pounding the Cape's shallow
and rocky shores — a graveyard for scores of ships —
claimed the vessel. Thankfully, all its passengers and
crew members made it ashore with the help of some
local people who rowed out to help.

But the lives of those aboard the wrecked ship weren't
the only ones saved that day. It had been a very
bleak year for families living along the Cape coast.
Food supplies had dwindled to the point that several
residents were actually starving, and by Christmas a few
had already died. So the local men who rowed out to

the wreck couldn't believe their eyes when they saw the ship's cargo. The *Moravian* had been carrying hundreds of barrels of apples and pickled pork, nearly 30 000 bushels of wheat, about 150 tons of bacon, nearly 50 tons of butter and more than 300 tons of cheese! After everyone was rescued, the men worked until dark salvaging all the food they could — plenty to feed the unfortunate passengers and crew for days, and more than enough to feed their own families for the rest of the winter.

He said What?

"The best way to treat a cold is with contempt."
— William Osler

Born at Bond Head, Canada West (now Ontario), in 1849, Osler became a world-famous doctor who dramatically changed the way medical students were taught.

Easy Does It

Often a simple idea turns out to be a great one. John Mitchell Lyons came up with one of those simple, great ideas when he was working as a railway clerk in Moncton, New Brunswick.

In the late 1870s, Moncton's train station was a very busy place. Trains were regularly arriving from and departing for several different destinations, and travellers often had to switch trains. But the busier the station got, the harder it was to keep track of luggage and make sure that it and its owners ended up in the same place at the same time.

Like so many other clerks across the country, Lyons often had to bear the brunt of travellers' complaints when they realized their bags were lost. But in 1881 he came up with a solution to the problem — a two-part baggage identification check that could be easily torn in half along a line of perforations. One half went to the passengers and the other was attached to their bags. Lyons patented his invention in 1882. It was such a simple, elegant and workable idea that versions of it are still being used around the world today.

Bear on Board

Being "boatjacked" by a bear was definitely not what Marty Descoteaux, owner of Elliot Lake Outfitters, had in mind when he promised visitors to his company's website "a world-class guided Ontario fishing adventure you will never forget." But that's what happened when he headed out one morning onto Esten Lake in his five-metre-long aluminum boat to see how well the fish were biting.

Fortunately, Descoteaux had no customers along for the ride that morning in July 2006, when a large bear swimming nearby suddenly decided it wanted to come aboard. When the bear reached up to grab the side of the boat, Descoteaux whacked it on the head with an oar, but that didn't stop it. When it pulled itself up and in, Descoteaux abandoned ship and started swimming for shore.

In the meantime the bear was checking out the boat, which was still moving at a slow, trolling speed. But when the hairy pirate bumped into the throttle of the main gas-powered motor, the boat shot forward. Descoteaux watched from shore as his craft headed toward some rocks. When it bumped into them, the bear was thrown into the water. It swam ashore and lumbered off into the woods, but the boat kept going, speeding around and around in circles for nearly half an hour until it ran out of gas.

Descoteaux's Ontario fishing adventure finally ended when he swam out and retrieved his boat. It was certainly an experience he would never forget, and it made for a great story to share with his clients when he took them fishing.

...that in 1940 Sudbury, Ontario, became the first city in Canada to install parking meters on its streets? Vancouver didn't begin installing the coin-hungry timekeepers until 1947, and Montreal held off until 1958.

A Parking Price Freeze

By the 2000s most Canadian cities were gradually replacing coin-operated meters with more efficient ways to collect payments for parking spots. But in Winnipeg, Manitoba, for a few days in the winter of 2007, new solar-powered pay stations gave people a break. When the temperature dropped below –30°C, their liquid crystal displays froze and they stopped issuing receipts for time paid. Instead of saving the city money the cold-sensitive kiosks cost Winnipeg about $2000 a day. Unlike the city's hardy residents, the new machines couldn't handle the cold.

Just the Stats In Canadian cities in the 1950s, a nickel could buy an hour of on-street metered parking. By 2006 the average hourly rate had reached $2.25.

Danger:
Escape Artist at Work

Wowing crowds with death-defying stunts is all part of a day's work for Dean Gunnarson of Winnipeg, Manitoba. What happened on Saturday, June 9, 2007, was no exception. That night about 2000 people attending the Old Tyme Country Fair in Niverville, Manitoba, watched and worried as two large tractors began a tug-of-war with Gunnarson, a captive human link at the centre of the ropes being pulled by the powerful machines.

As the tractors drove in opposite directions, slowly picking up the slack in the long ropes, Gunnarson worked feverishly to dismantle the trap he had set for himself — padlocked chains wrapped around his body and handcuffs clamping his hands together. Just as the rope from one tractor went taut and yanked him sideways, he escaped from the last of his restraints and the ropes. The crowd cheered, relieved that the master magician and escape artist hadn't been ripped apart in front of them.

But back in 1983, on Halloween, the thousands of Winnipeggers who had gathered to watch a young Gunnarson perform one of his earliest dramatic escapes had no cause to cheer. Gunnarson had been chained up, sealed in a coffin and thrown into the Red River. Then something went terribly wrong. Unable to escape his shackles, the young man was submerged in the chilly waters for four minutes before the coffin was pulled from the river and opened to rescue him. By that time, he was unconscious and turning blue.

That event was Gunnarson's closest brush with death, but not his most daring stunt. Over the years and around the world he has performed hundreds of amazing feats before TV cameras and huge crowds of appreciative fans. He has been thrown out of a plane handcuffed, chained and in a straitjacket — with just seconds to escape and open a parachute. He's been covered with chicken meat and dangled in restraints over a pit of dozens of hungry alligators. He's been chained to the tracks as a roller coaster thundered toward him. It's no wonder he's considered a master of the world's most dangerous magic, and one of the best escape artists in the world.

...that the prairie rattlesnake is the only poisonous snake slithering around the Canadian prairies? About a metre long, this greenish-grey or greenish-brown reptile can be found anywhere from southwestern Saskatchewan and southern Alberta to south-central British Columbia. Southern British Columbia is also home to Canada's only member of the boa family, the rubber boa, a constrictor that swallows its prey whole. But it's less than a metre long, just a tenth of the length of some other boas around the world such as pythons and anacondas, so the prey it swallows is pretty small.

The black rat snake is Canada's largest snake, reaching lengths of up to 2.5 metres. It's only found in southern Ontario. And one province, Newfoundland, doesn't have any naturally occurring snakes. It doesn't have any porcupines, raccoons, groundhogs or skunks either.

More Cross-Border Stardom

Three times in major league baseball history a Canadian has been named Most Valuable Player. Joey Votto of Toronto, Ontario, was named the National League MVP in 2010 while playing first base for the Cincinnati Reds. In 2006 Justin Morneau of New Westminster, British Columbia, a first baseman for the Minnesota Twins, was chosen as the American League's MVP. Nine years earlier, Larry Walker of Maple Ridge, B.C., was the 1997 choice for the National League's MVP while playing for the Colorado Rockies.

The year 2006 was also good for another great athlete from British Columbia — superstar basketball player Steve Nash. In 2006 Nash, who grew up in Victoria, was named the National Basketball Association's MVP for the second year in a row while playing for the Phoenix Suns.

What's that, eh?

There are a lot of jumpers in southern Alberta, Saskatchewan and Manitoba. They're found in New Brunswick, Nova Scotia, Quebec and Ontario too, but there they aren't called jumpers. This is the name given to the white-tailed deer by many people on the prairies, and it's a fitting name for these large herbivorous, or plant-eating, mammals. White-tailed deer are impressively athletic. From a standing start they can spring about 1.8 metres into the air, and from a running start they can soar to nearly 2.5 metres.

Quebec's Anticosti Island in the Gulf of St. Lawrence is home to about 130 000 white-tailed deer, making it a great place to visit if one is hoping to spot a jumper or two.

DID YOU KNOW... ...that a Canadian invented processed cheese?

James Lewis Kraft was born in Stevensville, a farming community in southern Ontario near Lake Erie. Growing up on a dairy farm and working as a clerk in the local grocery store, Kraft became interested in learning about ways to prevent cheese from spoiling. In 1903, when he was 29, he moved to Chicago and began selling cheese to grocery stores. A few years later four of his brothers joined him in Chicago and they formed a business called J.L. Kraft and Brothers. After that Kraft started experimenting with cooking up batches of melted cheese that wouldn't quickly spoil or go mouldy, and that could be sold in small tins. In 1916 he received a patent for the method he had come up with to produce processed cheese, and the Kraft brand on cheese soon became one consumers felt they could trust.

Super Old

A centenarian is someone who lives to be 100 years old. About one in 1000 centenarians lives to celebrate a 110th birthday too, and those who do are referred to as supercentenarians. On September 16, 2001, Julie Winnefred Bertrand of Montreal, Quebec, turned 110 and joined this special group.

Even more special — only one in 15 supercentenarians lives to be 114. Ms. Bertrand did that in September 2005. She even went on to celebrate her 115th birthday in September 2006, and when 116-year-old Elizabeth Bolden from Memphis, Tennessee, died in December 2006, Bertrand became the world's oldest woman and second-oldest person. At that time there were only 77 other verified supercentenarians alive.

Bertrand was born in Coaticook, a town in Quebec's Eastern Townships, not far from the Vermont, USA, border. There she worked most of her adult life as a buyer for a department store. In the 1970s she moved to a nursing home in Montreal. Bertrand never married, but at one time she did date a handsome young lawyer from a nearby town — Louis St. Laurent, who went on to serve as Canada's prime minister from 1948 to 1957.

Bertrand died in her sleep on January 18, 2007, just six days before she would have become the oldest person in the world.

Just the Stats

According to the numbers, Canadians, especially women, are living longer now. In the 1960s fewer than 20 people a year were centenarians when they passed away; in 2004, more than 300 were. The 2011 Canadian census counted 5825 living centenarians, 2030 more than in 2001, and five out of every six of them were women.

How Big Are They?

As some Quebecers say:

"At my grandmother's cottage, the mosquitoes are so big they have to kneel to bite us in the forehead."

That's big!

Man-Eating Mosquito

The town of Upsala, Ontario, northwest of Thunder Bay, must figure there's no point trying to hide the fact that some pretty big, bloodthirsty mosquitoes hang out in the area. Visitors there are met right up front with a monstrous member of that insect clan — a steel and fibreglass creature nearly five metres long. But this mosquito isn't just huge; it's really hungry too. Armed with a knife and a fork, it's just waiting to dig into the 1.8-metre-tall man it's clutching in its long, steely legs.

The Ice Patch Moccasin

In 2003 Cody Joe, a member of the Champagne and Aishihik First Nations, was working with an archaeological research team examining melting ice patches in the southern Yukon. The team was looking for early evidence of aboriginal peoples' presence in the area, so it was especially fitting that Cody Joe was the one who came across the brown, dirt-covered clump of animal hide that the researchers would find so interesting. Moss was growing out of it and it was covered with animal dung, but over the next two years Yukoner Valery Monahan worked for nearly 250 hours carefully cleaning, reconstructing and preserving the item. In February 2006 the territory's Ministry of Tourism and Culture was proud and pleased to announce an amazing discovery. What Cody Joe had found was a 1400-year-old moccasin — the oldest example of a First Nations moccasin ever found in Canada. The leather footwear was probably sewn together and worn by early Athapaskan people.

The Minister's New Shoes

The minister of finance is an important member of Canada's Parliament in Ottawa. Every year or so, it is his duty to present the budget — the government's major plans for spending taxpayers' money — in a speech in the House of Commons. Many Canadians think that, traditionally, he wears a new pair of shoes for the occasion. But is this true?

Researchers at the Library of Parliament spent a long time trying to get to the bottom of things, but came up empty-handed. They couldn't find when or why the new-shoe idea began, or any evidence that it had been around for very long. In fact, the library's research showed that the first time a newspaper reported that a minister of finance wore new shoes to present a budget was when Jean Chrétien did in 1978. Before that, all the way back to 1946, no minister of finance wore new shoes on budget day. And for the 26 budget speeches from 1978 until the spring of 2007, finance ministers wore new shoes just 11 times.

So, when it comes right down to it, there really isn't an old new-shoe tradition at all. But a few finance ministers who thought there was came up with their own personal approaches to the idea. In December 1979 minister of finance John Crosbie strode into the House of Commons to deliver his budget speech wearing a pair of mukluks, and in February 1994 Paul Martin wore a new pair of work boots. And for his March 2007 budget Jim Flaherty didn't buy new shoes for himself; instead, he bought a new pair of skates for his son.

What's that, eh?

If you hear the word *snotty* on Prince Edward Island, it might not mean what you think if you assume it's referring to a snobbish person or to the face of a little kid with a runny nose. An Islander might very well use *snotty* to describe a damp, grey day with a light rain falling. That's snotty weather on P.E.I.

DID YOU KNOW...

...that Gimli, Manitoba, on the southwestern shore of Lake Winnipeg, is home to the world's largest number of people of Icelandic descent outside Iceland itself? Immigrants from Iceland looking for a better life first began settling there in 1875, and the community has maintained a distinctive Icelandic culture to this day. The ever-popular Icelandic Festival of Manitoba has been held there in early August every year since 1932.

A Canadian Viking

In 1967 Gimli, Manitoba, chose to celebrate Canada's centennial — the country's hundredth birthday — by having a really big statue built. In keeping with its Icelandic roots, the town erected a 4.6-metre-high fibreglass Viking!

Thinking Big for the Fun of It

In the early 1990s Gladstone, Manitoba, about 150 kilometres west of Gimli, decided it wanted a big roadside attraction too, one that would welcome tourists travelling along the Yellowhead Trans-Canada Highway. In 1993, with a wink and a nod to the town's name, an 11-metre-high monument was built, topped by a huge, round, smiling fellow. His name? Happy Rock, of course. And to encourage travellers to drop in for a visit, the good people of Gladstone spread the word that it was good luck to get your picture taken under the statue of Happy Rock. Clever folks, those Gladstone residents, and with a sense of humour too.

Have Rock, Will Travel

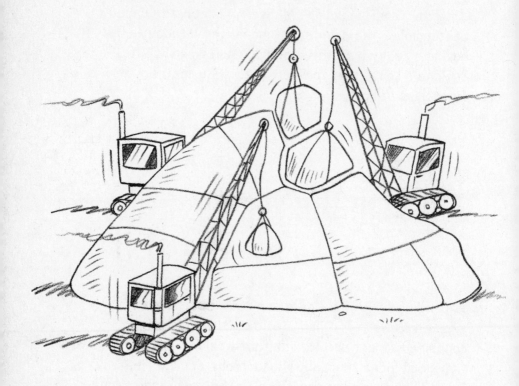

The Happy Rock monument in Gladstone is made of fibreglass and weighs about 1.4 tonnes. In the 1990s designers of a small park in Yorkville, Toronto's most fashionable shopping and dining district, also wanted a big rock to welcome tourists. But they wanted the real thing — a one-billion-year-old piece of granite that was located about 180 kilometres north of the city, and which weighed in at a whopping 650 tonnes.

Getting that rock to Toronto was a major challenge. First the top 2.1 metres of a massive area of weather-worn Canadian Shield granite had to be sliced off — in 135 manageable pieces weighing from about 225 to 900 kilograms. Each piece was labelled to show how it fitted with the others, and then a crane loaded the sections onto 20 flatbed trucks for the trip south. When the pieces arrived in Toronto, cranes unloaded them and workers guided them into their correct positions at the park site, wedging them together like pieces of a giant jigsaw puzzle. Then the joints were heat-sealed together to make the 19-metre by 15-metre rock's surface look like one solid piece again. Voilà! A bit of natural landscape transplanted to a bustling city street ...

DID YOU KNOW...

...that the first park in the world north of the Arctic Circle was Auyuittuq National Park on Nunavut's Baffin Island? There's no need to move any rocks to this vast park. It consists of nearly 20 000 square kilometres of towering granite mountains, up to 300-metre-deep ice fields and 900-metre-high coastal cliffs, or fjords. The park was established in 1976. Its name, Auyuittuq, is an Inuktitut word that means "land that never melts."

A Real Cutie

Melody and Carl-Richard Dancel, from Tecumseh, Ontario, thought their eight-month-old daughter, Cameron, was as cute as a button. But they had no idea she'd be considered contest-winning cute. However, Melody figured she had nothing to lose by entering a photo of their little girl in a "Beautiful Baby Search" competition being run by the *Live with Regis and Kelly* morning television show. On February 5, 2007, about an hour and a half before the contest's website stopped accepting entries, she posted a favourite picture of Cameron on-line, unaware that at least 150 000 other proud parents had entered photos too.

But a few weeks later, Melody ended up being the proudest and most excited parent of them all. She, her daughter and her husband were flown to New York City to appear live on the show — because Cameron had won the contest. Her prize? Her photo on the cover of the Summer 2007 issue of *Parenting* magazine, and $5000 toward her college education. Emily Saniga, a toddler from Toronto, Ontario, was another winner, receiving $1000 for placing fifth in the competition.

Debby Hits Forty — Party On!

In December 2006 a polar bear named Debby, one of the most popular residents of Winnipeg, Manitoba, turned forty. Orphaned soon after she was born in the Russian

Arctic and unable to survive on her own, Debby was just a few months old when she was sent to Winnipeg in the spring of 1967. She settled in to her new home at the Assiniboine Park Zoo and quickly became a hit with visitors. She grew up and met her mate, Skipper, there, and over the years the contented couple had six healthy baby bears. Skipper was 34 when he died in 2001, an unusually old age for a polar bear, but not nearly as unusual as Debby's. The average life span of a polar bear is about 15 years, and it's rare for one to make it past 20.

After Debby's 40th birthday, 17-year-old Samantha Machan decided to send news of that special event to Guinness World Records, and in August 2007, Machan and zoo officials learned that Debby had made it into the record book as the world's oldest living polar bear. Debby took the news in stride, doing what she usually did each day — curling up for a long nap.

He said What?

"If you don't protect your cabin or your house, you will have to redecorate."
— Reg Bell, elementary school student,
Churchill, Manitoba

Reg was referring to the mess a polar bear can make if it manages to break into a building in Churchill.

A Bear-y Safe Halloween

In Churchill, Manitoba, more than 1000 kilometres north of Winnipeg, people don't have to go to the zoo to see polar bears. In the fall the bears often wander into town looking for a snack. The males drop in on their way to the ice floes on Hudson Bay where they'll find plenty of seals to eat, and the females check out the place on their way to dens about 150 kilometres south where they'll give birth.

Tourists from around the world travel to Churchill for a chance to watch these magnificent creatures, but the last thing local parents want to see lumbering through town when their children are outside is a big, powerful, hungry polar bear. And Halloween is one day when kids definitely want to be out and about, even in the polar bear capital of the world. So, to make sure they can go trick-or-treating like other kids across the country, the town's polar bear patrol goes into action.

Starting on October 30, police, parks officials, firefighters, paramedics and volunteers make regular rounds of the town looking for bears. If they spot one, they try to scare it off with sirens and bright lights, but if that doesn't work, they shoot it with a tranquilizer gun. When it's sound asleep, they move it to a compound known as the polar bear jail until a helicopter can fly it far away from Churchill.

And when it comes to choosing a costume, dressing all in white is a definite no-no. You do not want to be mistaken for a bear that gets targeted with a tranquilizer dart. Wearing a seal costume isn't such a good idea either. If a hungry bear did manage to get past the patrols, it might find a young seal look-alike very tempting.

...that even though polar bears look white, the long hairs of their fur are actually transparent and colourless, like glass? And did you know that long hairs grow even on the bottoms of their paws, to help keep their feet warm and give them more grip on the ice?

Bigfoot Believer? Or Not?

On April 4, 2007, Mike Lake, Conservative Member of Parliament for the Edmonton-Mill Woods riding in Alberta, said that he didn't make judgment calls on petitions submitted to him by his constituents. But maybe he should have before agreeing to present one particular petition in the House of Commons on March 28, 2007. It asked the federal government to legally protect none other than the big, hairy beast known as Bigfoot — by granting it endangered species status.

Some people wondered aloud why a creature whose existence is questionable would need to be protected from becoming endangered. Others asked why Lake would waste Parliament's time with such an issue when

there were more important things for it — and him —
to worry about. When questioned, Lake said he didn't
personally support the petition, because he didn't
believe Bigfoot existed.

Prime Minister Harper's government had 45 days in
which to respond. Lake probably breathed a sigh of
relief when the government let the deadline pass
without taking any action.

Banking on the Future

When award-winning actor and comedian Jim Carrey was just a kid growing up in Newmarket, Ontario, he was already making his friends laugh with his jokes and silly routines. They thought he was really funny, and he did too, so when he was only 10 he dared to mail in an application to work on *The Carol Burnett Show*, a popular comedy hour on TV in the early 1970s.

Not surprisingly, Carrey didn't get the job, but he didn't get discouraged either. As an older teen, he was still so confident he'd make it in the entertainment business that he wrote himself a postdated cheque for $10 million, vowing to carry it around in his wallet until he had earned that much money.

Carrey moved to Los Angeles, California, in the early 1980s and after a lot of hard work he did make it big, doing so well as a comic and an actor that by late 1995, the date he had written on that cheque years earlier, he was actually worth $10 million. And by 1996 he was doing so very well that he was paid twice that much to star in just one film, *The Cable Guy*.

He said What?

"You miss one hundred per cent of the shots you never take."
— Wayne Gretzky, hockey superstar

The Most Valuable Player in Manitoba

On March 18, 2005, 66-year-old Phyllis Thomas of Peguis, Manitoba, stopped on her way to Winnipeg to watch a grandson play hockey and bought two lottery tickets. Later that evening, she scratched off the coating to reveal the numbers, and was amazed to discover that one ticket was a really big winner worth $1 million.

Two years later, on March 31, 2007, Thomas stopped on her way to Winnipeg to watch a grandson play hockey and bought two lottery tickets. Later that evening, she scratched off the coating to reveal the numbers, and was absolutely stunned to discover that she held another really big winning ticket — another one worth $1 million!

He said What?

"Would it be fair not to give the fans the chance to see my beautiful face?"

— Lorne "Gump" Worsley

Montreal-born Worsley was a hockey Hall-of-Famer who was a goalie in the NHL from 1953 to 1974. He played a total of 861 games, and only wore a mask for the last six of them.

What Time Is It, Anyway?

Canada is so wide that it's divided into six time zones: Pacific, Mountain, Central, Eastern, Atlantic and Newfoundland Standard Time. So there's a 4-hour time difference between places in British Columbia and Newfoundland. As well, each spring Canada switches to daylight saving time, which is one hour later than standard time. Since 2007 the switch happens on the second Sunday of March — and the country returns to using standard time on the first weekend of November.

So if you know about the time zones and daylight saving time, you shouldn't have any trouble figuring out what time it is. But . . .

. . . Saskatchewan doesn't switch to daylight saving time in the spring. Except for Denare Beach, Sturgeon Landing and Creighton, Saskatchewan, which do switch because folks there want to run on the same time as Flin Flon, Manitoba, during the summer months. Lloydminster, which is right on the Saskatchewan-Alberta border, switches too. And . . .

. . . Dawson Creek and Fort St. John in British Columbia stay on Mountain Standard Time all year long. That means they're actually on Pacific Standard Time during the summer when British Columbia switches to daylight saving time. And . . .

. . . Atikokan, Ontario, because it's west of the 90°W line of longitude, is supposed to keep Central Standard Time, but it stays on Eastern Standard Time all year long. That means in the winter it's using the same time as Thunder Bay, Ontario, and in the summer it's on the same time as Fort Frances and Rainy River when they're on Central Daylight Saving Time. And . . .

. . . with few exceptions, all places in Quebec east of the 63°W line of longitude are on Atlantic Standard Time. And . . .

. . . there are several more exceptions — which makes keeping track of keeping time in Canada sound very complicated. In most cases it's not, but probably the best answer to the question, "What time is it?" is, "It all depends on where you are."

Making Sure Everyone's On Time

Canada's provinces and territories all have laws that regulate what time it's supposed to be in each of their regions of the country. But some cities and towns, such as Atikokan, Ontario, most parts of Labrador, and Creighton, Saskatchewan, simply ignore those laws because they think life is easier if their residents are using the same time as nearby communities.

Many people living in Moosomin, Saskatchewan, work just across the border in Manitoba. They wish their town would switch to daylight saving time every spring, even though it's not supposed to. From spring to late fall, when the clock says 7 a.m. in their town, it says 8 a.m. in Manitoba. So while their neighbours who work in Saskatchewan are still sleeping, they're hustling to get to work!

Determined to make sure everyone in Alberta switched to daylight saving time each spring, that province's government actually passed a law in 2000 saying that "no person shall . . . use or observe within Alberta any time other than Daylight Saving Time," and that any person who doesn't "is guilty of an offence and liable to a fine not exceeding $25." One can't help wondering how officials would know if a person wasn't operating on daylight saving time. And if they did find some persons who weren't, would they keep fining them $25 over and over again if they refused to set their clocks forward an hour? Hmm . . .

IT'S LATER THAN YOU THINK IN SASKATCHEWAN, IF IT'S NOT REALLY AS EARLY AS YOU THINK IT IS IN MANITOBA!

IT'S STILL BEDTIME!

Canada's Four Corners

A quadripoint is a point on the earth that touches four distinctly separate regions of the world. A secondary quadripoint is a point where the boundaries of four political subdivisions, such as provinces or states, meet. There aren't very many quadripoints in the world, but there is one in Canada. It's located in the far north, at the southeastern end of Lake Kasba, which is mainly in the Northwest Territories. There the boundaries of Saskatchewan, Manitoba, the Northwest Territories and Nunavut meet at a point, like a four-corner intersection or crossing.

DID YOU KNOW...

...that Quebec is the only province that borders three other provinces? It touches both New Brunswick and Newfoundland and Labrador on the east, and it borders Ontario on the west.

Oops!
Wrong Direction!

Many Canadians make the mistake of thinking that if they want to go from Windsor, Ontario, to Detroit, Michigan, they have to head south. But Windsor, located at 42°18' N, is south of Detroit at 42°23' N. Check it out on a map.

The Western Giant

That's the nickname given to 1.94-metre-tall John "Jack" Hugh Gillis, who was finally inducted into British Columbia's Sports Hall of Fame in 2006 — 100 years after he arrived in Vancouver.

Soon after he settled there in 1906, Gillis joined the Vancouver Police Force. He also started entering — and winning — "All-Round" competitions, a combination of several track and field events a lot like decathlons today.

In 1909 he became the All-Round Champion of Canada, and the next year he placed second in the American All-Round Championship. As the holder of more than 60 medals in various events, he was really looking forward to doing well at the 1912 Olympics in Stockholm, Sweden, but was terribly disappointed when he fell ill and couldn't go. A year later, when he was just 29, he died, a victim of tuberculosis.

One of Gillis's shotput throws was so long it set a record that stood for 32 years. But Gillis, originally from Cape Breton, Nova Scotia, held another record that was even more impressive. It had to do with how he got to British Columbia. On February 3, 1906 — long before a network of roads connected east to west — he set out on foot from Sydney, Nova Scotia. He arrived in Vancouver nearly eight months later, on September 24. Gillis followed the train tracks whenever he could, but he didn't ride the rails. Instead, he became the first person ever to walk across Canada.

Just the Stats

In the summer of 2005, Canadians took 12.2 million trips to go swimming, 8.2 million trips to go boating and 6.4 million trips to go fishing. Canadians also spent $1.5 billion on plants for their gardens, buying nearly 570 million flowers and 465 million vegetables.

Playgrounds for All

Many Canadian families can't afford to head to the lake each summer to go swimming and boating, but the fun that kids can have on public playgrounds in every city and town across the country is free, thanks in part to the efforts of a New Brunswicker named Mabel Phoebe Peters.

Peters was born in Saint John, New Brunswick, in 1861. Her father ran a hotel there, and in the late 1800s she and her sister helped him run it. Peters was also very active in the early women's rights movement, and a strong believer in a community's responsibility to help families care for their children.

Seeing kids playing in the streets and getting into all sorts of mischief during summer holidays, she began a campaign in the early 1900s to get local councils to set up safe, publicly funded play areas.

In 1906, with help from a local newspaper editor, she gathered enough local support and donations to set up the Allison Ground Playground in Saint John, the first public playground in Canada. She then spent the next few years before her death in 1914 travelling to many Canadian cities, promoting the creation of playgrounds for all. It's still a great idea.

DID YOU KNOW... ...that the wettest city in Canada is Prince Rupert, British Columbia, with an average of just over 2590 millimetres of precipitation a year? Prince Rupert is also the cloudiest city, putting up with about 6150 hours of grey, overcast skies each year. But Prince Rupert faces its shortage of dry, sunny days head on, proudly assuming the title of Cloudiest and Wettest City in Canada.

Cold Summer – 1999

Prince Rupert residents may take their damp, grey days in stride, but folks in Calgary, Alberta, complained loudly about the summer of 1999. It wasn't just mainly damp and grey; it was also miserably cold. More snow fell in Calgary in July of that year than in February. On July 15 the daytime temperature plummeted to 2.7°C. With winds gusting to more than 50 kilometres per hour that day, it felt like -14°C at times — definitely not shorts weather.

She said What?

" 'Snow in April is abominable,' said Anne. 'Like a slap in the face when you expected a kiss.' "
— Lucy Maud Montgomery

The "Anne" in this quote is Anne Shirley, the unforgettable fictional character brought to life by Canadian author Lucy Maud Montgomery in *Anne of Green Gables*, published in 1908. Since then millions of readers around the world have fallen in love with Anne, and with her home province of Prince Edward Island.

Surely Anne would have sympathized with Calgarians during the summer of 1999. One can only imagine what words she would have used to describe snow in July — "devastating"? "unbearable"? Or perhaps she would have found such a possibility "utterly unspeakable" . . .

Warm Summer – 1999

But while Calgarians shivered in the west, many Newfoundlanders in the east enjoyed warmer-than-usual summer weather in 1999. It was so warm that, for only the second time in nearly a century, not a single iceberg drifted south of St. John's. They had all melted. Some years up to 1000 icebergs have made it that far south.

Live Long and Prosper:
Greetings from Vulcan

Vulcan, Alberta, about 130 kilometres southeast of Calgary, was originally named in the early 1900s after the Roman god of fire. But the name took on an added dimension with the phenomenal success of the *Star Trek* television series and films that featured pointy-eared aliens like Spock, Sarek and Tuvok from the planet Vulcan. Hoping to attract more tourists to their town, some real-life Vulcans decided to have a local welder named Gary McKinnon build a really big spaceship that looked very much like the TV show's famed starship, the USS *Enterprise*.

McKinnon finished the nearly 9.5-metre-long ship in June 1995. Impressive enough in the daytime, it's even more alluring at night when it's lit in such a way that it appears to be hovering above the ground at the entrance to the town. In the fall of 1998, the town added a 16-metre-tall space station that serves as the area's tourism centre and also features science fact-and-fiction displays of interest to visitors, especially Trekkies — extremely loyal *Star Trek* fans.

And Trekkies do make their way to Vulcan; in fact, hundreds of them, complete with costumes, turn up each year when the town plays host to the Spock Days *Star Trek* convention. In 2007 Vulcan added a popular new attraction in keeping with the *Star Trek* theme — a virtual reality game that lets players stand on the bridge of a starship and defend it from alien invaders (not Vulcans, of course).

257

Putting Out the
Welcome Mat for UFOs

The *Enterprise* look-alike starship "landed" in Vulcan, Alberta, on schedule in 1995. But about 600 kilometres north, people in St. Paul, Alberta, have been waiting since 1967 for a spaceship to land there.

Taking a lighthearted approach to choosing a Centennial project celebrating Canada's 100th birthday, some residents decided to show that St. Paul was such a visitor-friendly place it would even welcome travellers aboard UFOs — unidentified flying objects. So they had the world's first UFO landing pad — 12 metres wide — built right in the middle of town. Beside the pad they erected a sign with the following message:

> ## REPUBLIC OF ST. PAUL
> ### (STARGATE ALPHA)
> THE AREA UNDER THE WORLD'S FIRST UFO LANDING PAD WAS DESIGNATED INTERNATIONAL BY THE TOWN OF ST. PAUL AS A SYMBOL OF OUR FAITH THAT MANKIND WILL MAINTAIN THE OUTER UNIVERSE FREE FROM NATIONAL WARS AND STRIFE. THAT FUTURE TRAVEL IN SPACE WILL BE SAFE FOR ALL INTERGALACTIC BEINGS. ALL VISITORS FROM EARTH OR OTHERWISE ARE WELCOME TO THIS TERRITORY AND TO THE TOWN OF ST. PAUL.

Over the years UFOs seemed to have trouble locating St. Paul, though the landing pad did start luring a few more visitors off the highway. But the numbers zoomed

258

up in 1995 after the local Chamber of Commerce decided, just for the fun of it, to set up a 1-800 hotline number that people could call to report UFO sightings. Much to their surprise, the calls started coming in by the thousands, and not just to report seeing mysterious flying objects. People called about being abducted by aliens, about seeing spooky lights, and about finding bizarre crop circles, or cattle cut up and studied by aliens, in their fields.

The publicity possibilities were irresistible. In 1998 St. Paul decided to hold an international UFO conference, and 200 delegates came. They hosted another one two years later, and about 600 people came!

The wacky idea of building the big pad back in 1967 was finally paying off. Fans of aliens, if not aliens themselves, were landing in St. Paul, and residents welcomed them — and their tourist dollars — with open arms.

Just the Stats

According to the 2006 Canadian UFO Survey, 736 UFO sightings were reported to UFOlogy Research of Manitoba that year. About 650 of those strange apparitions turned out to be identifiable things such as planes, planets, and meteors, leaving about 85 sightings that couldn't be explained away so easily . . .

What ELSE Is Out There?

Actor James Doohan was born in Vancouver, British Columbia, and moved to Sarnia, Ontario, as a teenager. When he was just 19, he enlisted in the Canadian army, and was hit six times by machine gun fire during the D-Day invasion of Normandy. After recovering from his wounds, he learned to fly and served as an army pilot until the end of the Second World War.

After the war, Doohan became an actor, and it was in his fictional role as an officer aboard something much bigger than an airplane that he became a star on the hit TV series, *Star Trek*. Doohan played the part of Montgomery Scott, the inventive space engineer who kept the massive starship *Enterprise* running and regularly obeyed Captain Kirk's command to "Beam me up, Scotty." His Scotty character was such a hit with fans that many teenagers gave him credit for inspiring them to become engineers.

Doohan died at age 85 in 2005. Two years later his family honoured a request he had made in his will, and beamed him up into the sky. On April 28, 2007, aboard a rocket operated by a private company in Houston, Texas, some of Doohan's cremated remains were launched into space, a fitting final real-life journey for one who had so often boldly gone, in a fictional world, where no man had gone before.

Canadian Pizza Company Delivers — to Afghanistan!

In the fall of 2003 Corporal Patrick Cyr was serving with Canadian forces stationed in Kabul, Afghanistan. He kept in touch with his family back in Canada via emails. In one email to his brother, Michael, he mentioned that one of the things he missed was a good pizza. Reading that, Michael decided to send some pizza to his brother — and about 2000 other soldiers at the same camp.

As executive vice-president of Boston Pizza International, Michael had no problem getting people at his company excited about his plan. The firm's president, Michael Cordoba, loved the idea, seeing it as a great way to show support for members of Canada's armed forces. Company officials contacted military officials and arrangements were made to include a container loaded with pizza fixings on a transport plane leaving the Canadian Forces base in Trenton, Ontario, on October 31.

Two days later 2200 frozen pizza shells and all the sauce, cheese and toppings needed to dress them arrived in Kabul. On November 11 — Remembrance Day — kitchen staff at the base made and cooked the pizzas and "delivered" them to Patrick Cyr and his fellow soldiers, compliments of his brother and everyone else at Boston Pizza back in Canada, more than 10 500 kilometres away.

The Biggest Coin in the World

Speaking of pizzas, in early May 2007, the Royal Canadian Mint in Ottawa introduced a new maple leaf coin about the size of an extra-large pizza. The colossal coin, 53 centimetres across and more than 3 centimetres thick, isn't just too big to slip into a pocket; it's also too heavy, weighing in at a whopping 100 kilograms. And since it's made of 99.99 per cent pure gold, it's also a bit too expensive for most collectors to add to their Christmas gift wish list. The face value of the coin is $1 million, but the actual price one would have to pay is at least $4 million, based on the going rate for 28.35 grams (one ounce) of gold.

She said What?

"They told me I was going to have the tallest, darkest leading man in Hollywood. Naturally I thought of Clark Gable."

— Fay Wray

Actress Fay Wray, born in Cardston, Alberta, in 1907, said this when talking about being offered the leading lady role in the 1933 film classic, *King Kong*. Her dreamy leading man turned out to be a tall, dark, giant gorilla!

A Smash Hit

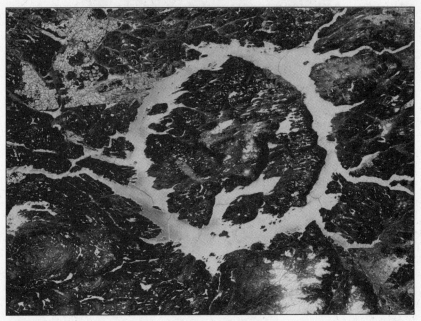

It's sometimes called "the eye of Quebec," and rightly so, because when seen from high above Earth, that's exactly what it looks like — a giant eye.

This amazing geological formation is the result of an event that happened more than 200 million years ago when a huge asteroid from outer space smashed into the rocky Canadian Shield of northern Quebec. When the asteroid hit, it sent intense shock waves through the rock, shooting broken pieces outward from the impact zone and leaving behind a massive crater about 100 kilometres across. Over millions of years the movement of glacial ice across the area scraped away the broken rock, scouring out a rim that filled with melting ice, creating an annular, or ring-shaped, lake called Lake Manicouagan. Like the white of an eye around the dark iris and pupil, the lake surrounds a large island — René-Levasseur Island.

Over a very long time erosion has shrunk the crater, known as the Manicouagan impact crater, but it's still 65 kilometres across, making it one of the five largest known impact craters on Earth. It so impressed astronaut Marc Garneau when he saw it from space that he nominated it for the Seven Wonders of Canada when the Canadian Broadcasting Corporation ran a competition asking Canadians to submit their choices.

Paddling Through History

Not everyone agreed with the results of the CBC's competition, but some folks at a museum in Peterborough, Ontario, were delighted to hear of one of the judges' seven choices.

From 1850 to 1960 several famous canoe factories were located in Peterborough, making it the world's centre for canoe building, and in 1997 the city also became home to The Canadian Canoe Museum, the largest canoe museum in the world. Its collection includes more than 600 canoes and kayaks of all shapes and sizes, as well as many other items associated with the history and uses of these lightweight boats so well suited to travel along Canada's vast network of waterways.

First Nations and Inuit people, whose ancestors were the original designers of these crafts, the many dedicated people who run and support the museum, and the museum's founder, University of Toronto professor Kirk Wipper, would all agree that the canoe deserves its place on the list of the Seven Wonders of Canada. So do millions of other Canadians.

And the Winners Were . . .

In 2007 tens of thousands of Canadians submitted dozens of selections, and the popularity of their choices helped the judges come up with the final list of Seven Wonders of Canada — a list that reflects both the natural and human history of the country.

Niagara Falls   Pier 21 in Halifax
The Rocky Mountains   The Igloo
The Prairie Skies   The Canoe
Old Quebec City

Just the Stats

There are more than 2.4 million paddlers — both canoeists and kayakers — in Canada.

A BIG Red Paper Clip

In 2006 Kipling, a town of about 1000 in southeastern Saskatchewan, installed something new in Bell Park — a 4.6-metre-long steel paper clip. It's painted bright red and it's strong enough for kids to climb all over if they want to, but that's not the main reason it was erected in Kipling. It may not be big enough to make it into the record books as the world's biggest paper clip, but it might be big enough to attract more visitors to town, especially during the annual Red Paper Clip Festival held in July.

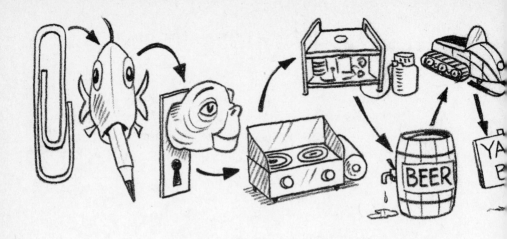

The REAL Red Paper Clip

It's hard to imagine why people would want to stop by to see a paper clip, even if it is a big one. But Kipling's connection with a real paper clip turned out to be a publicity dream come true.

On July 12, 2005, Montrealer Kyle MacDonald posted his willingness to trade a small red paper clip on an Internet site, hoping he would receive something better. Sure enough, someone offered him a fish-shaped pen and he made the trade. Then he offered to trade the pen, and accepted an E.T.-shaped doorknob (of *E.T.: The Extra-Terrestrial* film fame). He traded the doorknob for a Coleman stove, the stove for a gas-powered generator, the generator for a keg of beer and beer party, the beer for a snowmobile, the snowmobile for a trip to Yahk, British Columbia, the trip for a 1995 cube van, the

van for a recording contract, the contract for a rent-free apartment in Phoenix, Arizona, for a year, and the apartment for an afternoon with rocker Alice Cooper.

By then MacDonald's trading had attracted a lot of publicity both on-line and on TV and radio, and the millions of people following his story were really surprised when he traded away the afternoon with Cooper for a KISS (an American rock band) snow globe. However, one of the people who had heard about MacDonald's activities was actor and independent filmmaker Corbin Bernsen. He had offered MacDonald a part in a film as a possible trade item. MacDonald figured he should try to get something Bernsen would really like to have in return. He found out that Bernsen was a keen snow globe collector so he had deliberately traded "down" to the snow globe.

MacDonald got the movie role, and then offered to trade it, and that's when Kipling, Saskatchewan, came into the picture. The town offered MacDonald a house on Main Street in exchange for the movie role. MacDonald accepted — and in 2006 he and his wife moved there. Thanks to all the publicity he had received, MacDonald got a book contract and a film deal too.

The town held local auditions for the movie role. Corbin Bernsen showed up and gave 19-year-old Nolan Hubbard from Kipling a part in his film, *Donna on Demand*. Bernson also started making plans to film his next movie, *3 Day Test*, in Kipling, and to use several local people in it.

So, in the end, MacDonald traded a small, red plastic paper clip for a house, and Kipling, Saskatchewan, got a big, red steel one that kids can climb on.

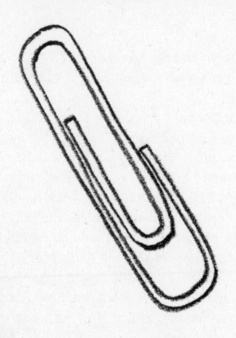

DID YOU KNOW...

...that in terms of the value of the diamonds mined, Canada is the third largest diamond producer in the world? The first Canadian diamonds were found around Lac de Gras in the Northwest Territories in 1991. As of 2013 there were four diamond mines operating in the NWT, one in Nunavut, and a sixth in northern Ontario.

Multi-Million-Dollar Penguins

Lane Merrifield, Dave Krysko and Lance Priebe, three dads from Kelowna, British Columbia, figured one way to make sure preteens could have a safe place to "hang out" on the Internet was to design one themselves. So, in 2005, they launched a subscription website called Club Penguin, populated by lovable virtual penguins whose activities encouraged kids to have fun and be creative in an ad-free space.

The founders' timing couldn't have been better. Two very successful films about penguins were released around the same time — *March of the Penguins* in 2005, and *Happy Feet* in 2006. The club proved to be such a hit that by 2007 it had 700 000 paying "members" worldwide, and the company was employing a staff of 100 in Kelowna. Wealthy investors began to make offers to buy the company, but it wasn't until one promised to keep Club Penguin ad-free and leave its headquarters in Kelowna that the three founders decided to sell. The buyer? The Walt Disney Company! And the selling price? A cool $350 million, with a promise of up to $350 million more by the end of 2009 if the number of subscriptions kept growing as predicted.

Multi-Million-Dollar Shoes

Another British Columbia parent, Sandra Wilson, wanted to find some comfortable shoes that would stay on her 18-month-old son's chubby little feet. She also wanted to find work that would let her spend as much time as possible with young Robert when her maternity leave ended. So she came up with a plan to design soft-soled leather booties — the kind of shoes she wished she could find for Robert — and to start working at home in North Vancouver making lots of them to sell to other parents.

Her plan worked, her designs were great, and to make a long success story short, Robeez Footwear Limited — the home-based company she started in 1994 — became so successful that by 2006 it had sales topping $15 million and employed nearly 400 workers. On September 6, 2007, Wilson agreed to sell her company to a major American shoe retailer, The Stride Rite Corporation, for $30.5 million. On the same day that she said goodbye to Robeez Footwear, she waved goodbye to her son Robert as he headed off to his first day at high school — 13 years after she had named her company after him.

Bidding Harry a Fond Farewell

In early August 2007, just a few weeks after *Harry Potter and the Deathly Hallows* hit the bookstores, Toronto, Ontario, played host to the world's largest Harry Potter conference, Prophecy 2007.

About 1500 fans and scholars from around the world — no one under 14 allowed — gathered in the Sheraton Centre downtown for four days of lectures, discussions, film screenings, quidditch games, wizardry duels, costume balls and quiet time spent in the Hall of Reflection, looking fondly back on a ten-year-long journey spent with Harry and sadly remembering beloved characters who died along the way.

A magically fantastic time was had by all. Long live Harry Potter!

He said What?

"The only time money is important is when you haven't any."
— Max Bell

Albertan George Maxwell Bell was a successful businessman, newspaper publisher and owner of many winning thoroughbred horses. He was also a generous philanthropist, donating a lot of money to many good causes. In 1977, five years after his death, Bell was named to the Canadian Horse Racing Hall of Fame.

They're at the post!
They're off!
She wins!

On September 14, 2001, Emma-Jayne Wilson wrote on a piece of paper, "I, Emma-Jayne Wilson, promise — promise — to make it as a jockey." Nearly six years later, on June 24, 2007, the 148th running of the Queen's Plate took place at Woodbine racetrack in Toronto, Ontario. One of the horses running in that race was Mike Fox, and the jockey riding him was Emma-Jayne Wilson. Mike Fox came from behind in the last 70 or so metres to win Canada's most important race for thoroughbreds, and Wilson made horse-racing history, becoming the first female jockey to ride a Queen's Plate winner across the finish line.

Students Outsmart Smarties' Maker

In the fall of 2005 Tanja Coghill, a teacher in Thunder Bay, Ontario, noticed that one fun fact printed on a box of Smarties claimed that Canadians ate four billion Smarties a year — enough Smarties to circle the world 350 times. Coghill decided that checking that fact would be a great math assignment for her Grade 6 students.

The students measured the sugar-coated chocolate candies made by Nestlé and learned that the diameter of each was one centimetre. That meant that four billion of them laid end to end would be four billion centimetres — or 40 000 kilometres — long. But when they found out that the circumference of Earth is about 40 000 kilometres, they realized something was wrong with the fact printed on the box. If the four billion number was right, Canadians ate enough Smarties each year to circle the world just once, not 350 times. And if the 350 times number was right, Canadians would have to eat one trillion four hundred billion Smarties a year!

Either way, the students figured out that the information on the candy box needed revising. They wrote three letters to the Nestlé company pointing out the error before they got an answer back telling them that in 2006 it would be dropped from the Smarties packages sold in Canada.

She said What?

"If you're not annoying somebody, you're not really alive."
— Margaret Atwood

Margaret Atwood was born in Ottawa, Ontario, in 1939, and grew up in northern Ontario and Quebec. An internationally renowned, award-winning author and poet, she's also been an outspoken supporter of many worthwhile causes.

DID YOU KNOW... ...that the section of Ontario's Highway 401 which runs through Toronto is the busiest stretch of road in North America?

Also known as the MacDonald-Cartier Freeway, the major transportation artery stretches nearly 820 kilometres east from Windsor, Ontario, to the Ontario-Quebec border, most of it as a four-lane divided highway. But in the Toronto area the roadway is 12 to 20 lanes wide in some places and carries more than 400 000 vehicles a day.

Between 2001 and 2006 the Royal Canadian Mounted Police force spent an average of $11.6 million a year on uniforms. There are 121 items included in the outfit needed to dress each officer, including four different types of hats, seven different kinds of footwear and six types of coats or jackets. And since 2001, even though most Mounties don't ride horses any more, the force has bought nearly $400 000 worth of spurs.

Monster Tooth

When nine-year-old Mark Henry of Francis Lake, Ontario, left the dentist's office one day in 2005, he had lost a tooth and gained a world record. The incisor the dentist had to pull to make room for another tooth trying to grow in Mark's mouth turned out to be super huge, as human teeth go. It was a whopping 2.28 centimetres long and 1.2 centimetres wide, the largest human tooth on record.

Gopher Problems

The small town of Torrington, Alberta, about 120 kilometres north of Calgary, has had a gopher problem for a long time. The gophers (actually Richardson's ground squirrels) are furry brown rodents about 30 centimetres long. They burrow extensive tunnels, leaving behind mounds of dirt and holes that can break the legs of cows. They're also hungry little vegetarians, dining on field crops and vegetable gardens, munching up to 60 per cent of their body weight every day. So farmers in the area feel they have to keep the gopher population under control. That means killing some of them.

When the Alberta government started a grant program in 1995 to help small towns come up with ways to attract more people, Torrington decided to look on the bright side of its gopher problem and apply for money to set up the world's first gopher museum. The grant money came through and the Torrington Gopher Hole Museum opened in June 1996 — to a flurry of controversy.

The museum displays six dozen stuffed (by a taxidermist) gophers dressed in detailed costumes and posed to look like the types of people you might find living and working in and around the town. When some animal rights groups heard about the museum's "residents" they began a campaign to stop people from visiting, saying displaying animals this way disrespects them, even if they are dead. Various papers and magazines ran stories about the controversy, and letters of complaint arrived at the museum from as far away as Germany, England and Japan.

But letters of support started coming too, and to the amazement of the 200 or so human residents of Torrington, so did visitors — several thousand a year since the tiny one-room museum opened in 1996!

The Case of the Missing Cheese

In October 2004 La Fromagerie Boivin, a cheese-making company in La Baie, Quebec, dropped 10 barrels of aging cheddar into the very deep, chilly waters of the Saguenay Fjord, near Tadoussac, Quebec. Luc Boivin, the firm's vice-president, decided to submerge the 800 kilograms of cheese, worth more than $40 000, in the hope that it would develop a tasty new flavour ripening under the high pressure exerted by the water.

But when Boivin came back in the summer of 2005 to pull up the cheese, he couldn't find it. After spending nearly $40 000 hiring divers with high-tech equipment to look for the sunken cheese, Boivin finally gave up the search. Did strong currents send the anchored barrels down the Saguenay River into the St. Lawrence? Did some lucky people fishing in the area snag a barrel and secretly return to make off with the rest? Or is the cheese still hiding deep in the fjord, ripening into the tastiest cheese ever made? The mystery of the missing cheese is a cold case, still waiting to be solved.

What's that, eh?

Skunky is a Canadian adjective used mainly to describe beer that's gone "off" and that tastes and smells foul. The word *skunk* itself comes from an Abenaki First Nation word *segongw*. The word *moose* is also Abenaki in origin, coming from the word *mos*.

Just the Stats

A 2.4-kilogram chicken produces about 100 grams of manure a day. A 195-kilogram pig eliminates just under 20 kilograms daily and a milk-producing cow weighing about 625 kilograms produces about 69 kilograms a day. That's a lot of poop! Fortunately, it can be recycled as fertilizer.

More Stats

In 2006 Canadian hens produced 588.4 million dozens of eggs. Canadians eat an average of 150 eggs per year.

Spuds Rule

The rich red soil of Prince Edward Island is ideally suited to the growing of potatoes. Farmers have been growing them there since 1790. The tiny province now produces about 1.29 million tonnes of potatoes each year, about one-third of all the potatoes produced in Canada. So what better place to erect a giant potato than on beautiful P.E.I.?

The giant fibreglass spud — 4.27 metres tall and 2.1 metres wide — proudly stands at the entrance to the Prince Edward Island Potato Museum in O'Leary, about 110 kilometres northwest of Charlottetown.

Would You Believe Potato Fudge?

Yes, potato fudge! Here's a recipe for it from Spud Island, P.E.I.'s nickname.

240 mL (1 cup) hot, lump-free mashed potatoes
1 pinch of salt
30 mL (2 tablespoons) butter
950 mL (4 cups) icing sugar
950 mL (4 cups) unsweetened coconut
2.5 mL (1/2 teaspoon) vanilla extract
120 mL (1/2 cup) semi-sweet chocolate, melted
120 mL (1/2 cup) maraschino cherries, chopped
and drained (optional)
60 mL (1/4 cup) nuts (optional)

Spread the hot potatoes on the bottom of a large bowl and sprinkle the salt on them.
Spread the butter over the potatoes until it melts.
Add all the other ingredients except the chocolate, and mix them together well.
Press the mixture into a 23 x 33 centimetre (9" x 13") pan.
Drizzle the melted chocolate over the top.
Allow the fudge to set. (This may take a few hours.)
When it's hardened, cut into squares.

Bon appétit!

Eh –
What's that, eh?

Adding *eh* to show that you understand, as in "So, it's really far away, eh ..." or that you agree with what someone's just said, as in "Right on, eh" is a distinctly Canadian use of this two-letter English word. It's also used to connect parts of a "story" you're telling, as in, "First, I got my bike, eh, and then I took off, eh, and ..."

English speakers in Ontario, Manitoba and New Brunswick use it way more, eh, than people in the rest of the country. However, in 2007 a University of Toronto language researcher, Sali Tagliamonte, released a study, eh, and it showed that people in Toronto weren't using it very often anymore, especially not younger people.

So, *eh* may be on the way out, eh. But, then again, many newcomers like using it to sound really Canadian, eh. So you never know, eh, what'll happen to *eh* ...

The smallest...

book in the world was produced in May 2007, by Li Yang and Karen Kavanagh, two physicists doing research at Simon Fraser University in Burnaby, British Columbia.

Titled *Teeny Ted from Turnip Town*, it's a fable written by a Canadian artist named Malcolm Douglas Chaplin. The 30-"page" book, just 0.07 millimetres by 0.10 millimetres, is about 20 times smaller than the head of a pin. It was "written" using a focused beam of fast-moving ions, or charged atoms, which "scrapes" just a few layers of atoms off a surface to create the teeny letters.

Yang and Kavanagh produced 100 copies of the book, and anyone with $20 000 can buy a copy. But you can't read it without a special kind of electron microscope, and one of those can cost hundreds of thousands of dollars. So *Teeny Ted from Turnip Town* isn't about to top the bestseller list any time soon. And there's no point looking for it at the local library, not even with a really powerful magnifying glass.

The world's first...

coloured coin put into circulation was the Canadian quarter featuring a red poppy on one side.

The attractive 25-cent piece honouring Canada's war veterans and the 117 000 Canadians who died serving their country made its debut in October 2004 at the Royal Canadian Mint's facilities in Winnipeg, Manitoba. About 30 million of the coins were distributed about two weeks before Remembrance Day on November 11.

To produce the coins, the Mint came up with a new process that applied red paint to the metal well enough that it was supposed to last for one to three years in circulation. Unfortunately, the colour faded or wore off more quickly than expected. But many Canadians chose to save, not spend, the quarters, keeping them as souvenirs of Remembrance Day and keeping the poppies on them red.

If at First You Don't Succeed

The Mint issued another red poppy quarter in October 2008, this time to commemorate the 90th anniversary of the end of the First World War.

These coins — 11 million of them — were also put into circulation just before Remembrance Day. They had gone through a special heating process to "bake" the red paint on the metal so it wouldn't fade the way it had on the 2004 quarters.

Danger! Spy Coins at Work

When the story broke early in 2007, it sounded like something straight out of a James Bond movie. The U.S Department of Defense had issued a warning that certain Canadian coins were a threat to the security of the United States. Reporters with the Associated Press news service tracked down more information about the strange warning and published their findings in May 2007.

Apparently a few American contractors suspected they were being spied on when they made business trips to Canada late in 2005. Because they were working on classified projects for the United States army, they filed reports about their worries with the U.S Department of Defense. And the reason for their suspicions? Some unusual coins with a micro-thin coating had turned up in their pockets and in a rented car. They couldn't identify the hard, clear coating on the coins, but they figured it must be part of a new miniature device that was sending out secret radio signals that could be used to track their movements.

If the Defense Department officials had had the coins tested, they would have found that they weren't emitting any radio signals. They would have recognized the coins as the red poppy quarters that Canada put into circulation in 2004. And they would have realized that the sinister "mysterious coating" was simply a covering over the red paint to stop it from wearing off.

Even if the 25-cent pieces had been tracking devices, how well would they have worked? What good would they have been if the people being spied on had spent them on a cup of coffee or slipped them into a parking meter, and gone merrily on their way?

Getting Squirrelled

Most golfers do everything they can to avoid the golf course hazards deliberately put in place to test their skills. But, in 2004, players at the Riverside Golf Course in Edmonton, Alberta, couldn't seem to find a way around one hazard that had been testing their patience — not how well they played — for several years.

The 10th and the 18th holes were especially hazardous that year. If golf balls landed on the greens there, they might never be seen again, because lurking in the bushes were some sneaky little squirrels that would zip across the grass, pick them up and make off with them before their owners arrived. Even if golfers arrived in time to catch the bushy-tailed thieves red-handed, there wasn't much point in running after them. They knew how ridiculous a human looked chasing a tiny ball-stealing squirrel, especially since the speedy little devils always got away.

Apparently the squirrels stockpiled most of the balls in birds' nests and forgot about them. The ones they remembered — or hadn't stored yet — they chewed on, gnawing off the hard outer layers of plastic right down to the rubber core. But they didn't eat the plastic; they spat it out and kept on chewing. They must have figured that golf balls helped them practise good dental hygiene.

Like beavers and other rodents, squirrels' teeth keep on growing; otherwise, they'd be worn right down gnawing through tough things like tree branches and nutshells. But if rodents don't chew enough, their teeth grow too long. Gnawing on something hard — like a golf ball — grinds down the teeth to keep them at just the right length.

Roadside Rodent

Beaverlodge, Alberta, is a small town about 40 kilometres west of Grand Prairie. In 2004, to celebrate the 75th anniversary of its incorporation, the town decided to put up a welcoming symbol of Beaverlodge at the entrance to the town. And the symbol they chose was — surprise, surprise — a beaver, a really big beaver sitting on a really big log.

At 5.5 metres long, 3 metres wide and 4.6 metres high, the long-toothed, beady-eyed rodent is the biggest beaver in the world.

And it's not surprising to find a 9.8-metre-tall moose named Mac standing beside the highway into Moose Jaw, Saskatchewan, and 8.5-metre-long Ernie the Turtle greeting visitors to Turtleford, Saskatchewan.

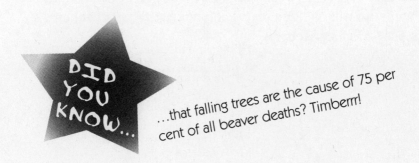

DID YOU KNOW...

...that falling trees are the cause of 75 per cent of all beaver deaths? Timberrr!

ORCA FM

In 1998 the first all-whale radio station in the world started broadcasting killer whales' clicks, moans and whistles from Johnstone Strait on the northeast coast of Vancouver Island.

The signal was strong enough to let people aboard nearby whale-watching boats listen in on the whales' underwater conversations. The sounds were also available to the listening public at 88.5 on the FM dial, thanks to the efforts of John K.B. Ford, a marine scientist studying whale sounds in Johnstone Strait. He had applied for a radio licence in 1997 to broadcast the sounds he was picking up on an underwater microphone as part of his research.

Bye-Bye, Boardwalk –
Bonjour, Montreal

In 2008 Hasbro, the toy and game company that makes Monopoly, introduced a new global edition of the game, Monopoly Here and Now: The World Edition. To give the game an international flavour, the company decided that the coloured property spaces would be cities — not streets — from around the world. But they let Monopoly fans decide which cities to choose, inviting them to vote on-line for their favourite metropolis. Five million ballots were cast, and the cities were ranked according to the number of votes they got. The top 22 became the new properties, and their ranking determined how much they would be worth.

Montreal, Quebec, got the most votes so it's the most expensive property on the World Edition. Vancouver and Toronto also made it to the new board, indicating either that Canadian cities are very popular with Monopoly fans worldwide or that Canadians really like voting on-line!

The highest...

streetcar line in the world that crosses a river runs along the High Level Bridge spanning the North Saskatchewan River in Edmonton, Alberta. It's 46 metres high!

A trip aboard one of the old-fashioned streetcars that rolls along the line isn't just a way for residents to cross the river — it's also a popular tourist attraction. The ride in a vintage tram is great fun, and the view is breathtaking.

But being so high up on such a narrow track with no barriers or guardrails on either side can be a bit too breathtaking for some people. It's not unusual for a few riders to keep their eyes tightly closed for most of the trip.

High-Wire Act

Anyone nervous about riding across Edmonton's High Level Bridge in a streetcar probably doesn't even want to think about dangling in a gondola, or cable car, nearly half a kilometre above the ground.

But that's the experience awaiting riders aboard the cable cars connecting two mountains that tower above the world-famous ski resort at Whistler, British Columbia. Known as the Whistler Blackcomb Peak 2 Peak Gondola, the cable car system that cost $52 million opened in December 2008.

The actual wire rope that carries the cars is 5.6 centimetres thick and stretches just over three kilometres between two of the tall metal towers, or pylons, that support it, the longest free span in the world. Twenty-eight cars travel across the valley at 7.5 metres a second, and the crossing takes 11 minutes. And if any gondola trip that high and long weren't exciting enough, two of the 28 cars offer riders an extra thrill — the middle sections of their floors are made of glass.

... that until midnight, December 31, 1921, British Columbians drove on the left side of the road? And did you know that Nova Scotians didn't switch to driving on the right until 2 a.m. on April 15, 1923?

Summertime Suppertime

Lip-Smacking Good

Shediac, New Brunswick, is a town just east of
Moncton on the shore of Northumberland Strait. About
5500 people live in the town, but every year, during
the first week of July, nearly 50 000 visitors show up.
They come to watch parades, listen to great Maritime
musicians, ride the latest midway attractions and swim
in the warmest salt water north of Virginia. But most of
all, they come to feast on the hard-shelled, big-clawed,
beady-eyed, antenna-waving seafood treasure for which
Shediac is famous. They come to eat lobster — served
up at lobster suppers held each evening of the Lobster
Festival.

Each night three visitors are chosen to enter a lobster-
eating contest. The winner is the fastest one to crack
open, pull apart and eat three lobsters — using bare
hands alone. The cheering crowds love watching the
messy race to reach the tasty flesh inside, and the
three volunteers are more than willing to entertain them
— because in this contest even the losers win. They get
to eat three lobsters for free.

And while they're in the Lobster Capital of the World, most visitors also check out the huge concrete sculpture in the park at the west end of town — a 5-metre-wide and nearly 11-metre-long 50-tonne lobster poised to give a 1.8-metre-tall fisherman a mighty big claw hug. The huge crustacean is the biggest lobster in the world. Nearly half a million people stop to look at it each year. And quite a few of them also drop by Shediac's other big sculpture — a huge white rooster in front of a fried chicken restaurant.

Save Big Dee-Dee

Another big lobster drew crowds to Shediac, New Brunswick, early in July 2008, when Denis Breau, owner of The Big Fish seafood shop and market, announced that he was going to auction off a very rare catch — a 100-year-old monster lobster weighing 10 kilograms. Breau set the starting bid at $1000, figuring some large restaurant might want to pay big bucks for it as a publicity stunt. The lobster's size and the high starting bid made the news, and within two weeks more than 1000 visitors had dropped by The Big Fish to see the big catch, which had been nicknamed Big Dee-Dee.

But as news spread that Big Dee-Dee was probably destined for a big pot of boiling water, an Internet campaign to save the huge lobster began, attracting the kind of publicity Denis Breau could have done without. The last thing he had wanted was to be seen as a greedy animal-hater, ready to end the life of a senior citizen of the sea, but some harassing phone callers were treating him as if that's exactly what he was.

Laura-Leah Shaw, a real estate agent from Vancouver, British Columbia, offered to buy Big Dee-Dee for $1000, along with two other anonymous bidders from Ontario who were ready to kick in $2000, just so the captive crustacean could swim free. As more offers came in, reporters from as far away as Europe started taking an interest in Big Dee-Dee's fate. But Breau decided he'd had enough of being caught in the media spotlight. He changed his mind about selling the mega lobster to the highest bidder, and arranged for him to live out the rest of his days in the comfort of an aquarium at the Huntsman Marine Science Centre in St. Andrews, New Brunswick. Here Big Dee-Dee could still be a big tourist attraction, but Breau wouldn't be, and that was fine with him.

We Can't Believe It Finally Looks Like Butter

In the summer of 2008, after 21 years of being the only province in Canada where making or selling yellow-tinted margarine was still illegal, the Quebec government finally lifted the ban against *la margarine jaune*. Before then, if Quebecers preferred spreading a sunny-coloured version of the popular non-dairy product on their muffins, they had to sneak it into the province.

Until the 1960s, yellow-coloured margarine had been banned in many places around the world, mainly because dairy farmers argued that its introduction would seriously cut into sales of butter. It was easier to spread and

Margarine or Butter?

a lot less expensive. The ban was also an attempt to stop crooks from selling "fake" butter — high-priced margarine made and packaged to taste and look like butter, and priced like it too. But by 2008 the Quebec government figured people could tell the difference and were entitled to make their own choice about the colour of the spread melting on their warm toast.

A Slam Dunk

The high school basketball game played in Toronto on February 7, 2002, between teams from West Hill Collegiate and R.H. King Academy was a blowout. West Hill won 150-58, thanks to the amazing play of a 1.96-metre-tall player named Denham Brown. Brown was hot that night. He sank 13 three-pointers! By the end of the first quarter he had scored 40 points. He scored another 41 in the third quarter, and by the end of the game, had chalked up a grand total of 111 points — the highest number of points ever scored by a Canadian basketball player.

Grab a Shovel

According to Environment Canada, more snow falls in Toronto on Thursdays than on other days of the week, and a one-day snowfall of more than 10 centimetres is unusual.

But in January 1999 something unusual happened. Starting with a 39-centimetre snowfall on January 2 and a 26-centimetre one on January 14, by the end of the month the city had received 118.4 centimetres, the heaviest one-month snowfall ever recorded for Toronto.

In fact so much snow fell that the city was having trouble keeping downtown streets clear and finding places to put the plowed snow. When emergency vehicles couldn't navigate the clogged streets, Mayor Mel Lastman called in the armed forces to help city workers with the cleanup. Nearly 450 troops and close to 130 military vehicles arrived from Petawawa, Ontario, and Prince Edward Island lent the city 15 big snow blowers. It took nearly two weeks for Toronto to dig itself out, and snow-clearing costs for the month totalled a whopping $70 million.

Planning Ahead

Some people living in Montreal and Ottawa made fun of Toronto for calling in the army to help them cope with the snow in January 1999. These cities are used to dealing with heavier snowfalls and proud of the very efficient snow-clearing plans they have in place.

Churchill Falls, Labrador, one of the top 10 snowiest places in Canada, has one of the coolest plans for dealing with snow removal. In the late 1960s, when permanent homes were built for employees of the massive new hydroelectric power station here, they were located on only one side of each street. That leaves plenty of space on the opposite side to push the metres of plowed snow that build up over the winter.

GHOULISH SCHOOL SUPPLIES

Back in the 1870s, several students attending medical school at McGill University in Montreal, Quebec, were often short of funds to pay their tuition fees. As well, back then, the medical school was often short of the corpses that students dissected to learn everything they could about human anatomy. So, to make extra money, some students would slip into the cemetery on the west side of Mount Royal late at night, dig up the bodies of poor people who had died recently, and sell them to the college for up to $50 each — a lot of money back then.

But before the students took the bodies away, they removed the clothes they'd been buried in. Anyone caught stealing bodies simply had to pay a fine because corpses weren't considered property. But stealing property such as clothes and shoes was criminal, and the body snatchers didn't want to be charged with and convicted of theft.

Ghostly Blame

Some people believe that the cemeteries on Montreal's Mount Royal are haunted. Apparently ghosts have been seen drifting around the boundaries of the burial grounds, and over the years there have been reported sightings of a ghost flying down the mountainside on a toboggan. The following paragraph might explain why such a spooky story came to be associated with that location. It's part of a description that a highly respected physician and anatomy professor, Dr. Francis J. Shepherd, wrote about how bodies arrived in his dissecting lab during the winter months in 1870:

"*The students went up at night, disinterred the bodies buried usually the previous morning, removed all clothing, wrapped them in blankets and tobogganed them down Côte des Neiges Hill. Many weird tales are told of accidents and the bodies rolling off the toboggan, and people who saw the accident thinking a death had occurred.*"

No wonder weird tales were told and rumours about toboggan-riding ghosts began to spread.

But on a more serious note, people may have found it easier to blame supernatural activity than to accept that Montreal and other Canadian cities didn't have a proper, respectful system for making corpses available to medical schools. Such a system was put in place in Canada in 1883, and by the next year grave-robbing for medical studies had come to an end.

Seating 10 000 People — 6 at a Time

Those words are on a sign outside the church in Drumheller, Alberta, known simply as The Little Church. At just 2.1 metres long and 3.4 metres wide, it may very well be the smallest church in the world. It is a tourist attraction, but it's also a place of worship, and anyone hoping to have a really, really small wedding might want to check it out. It has just six one-person pews, and there's barely enough room for the happy couple and the minister to stand at the front.

One-of-a-Kind Dinosaur Find

Drumheller, Alberta, has another tourist attraction that draws much bigger crowds than The Little Church does. Located about 140 kilometres northeast of Calgary, the town gets nearly half a million visitors each year because it's home to the world-famous Royal Tyrrell Museum of Paleontology. The museum displays one of the world's finest collections of dinosaur fossils. The town is also home to the world's largest dinosaur — a model that people can climb inside. Nine storeys tall, the T-rex towers above the surrounding badlands. Several much smaller sculptures of other dinosaurs, such as Triceratops and Stegosaurus, are located in the town itself, providing tourists with some great photo ops. Two of those sculptures are particularly interesting. They depict Smileasaurus Banana Eater and Shysasaurus Jelly Bean Eater, dinosaurs so rare that no one outside Drumheller had ever heard of them before their statues were revealed. Their skeletons were discovered deep in the imagination of an artist with a good sense of humour.

Big Art on Display

Trygve "Tig" Seland, a contractor and artist who lived in Drumheller, created many of the dinosaur sculptures placed around his hometown. He also designed and erected The Little Church.

But Drumheller isn't the only place in Alberta where you can see examples of Seland's artistic efforts. He designed Aaron, the 2.4-metre-high great blue heron that welcomes visitors to Barrhead, a small town in northern Alberta. He also designed three large sculptures of magnificent grey geese taking off, flying and landing in Hanna, and Eddie, a 2.4-metre-tall red squirrel in Edson.

East Coast Boast

People live longer in Nova Scotia than in other parts of Canada. More people get to celebrate their 100th birthday here, especially in Lunenburg and Yarmouth, than in any other place in the country. On average, 14 to 15 per 100 000 Canadians reach that major milestone, but as many as 50 per 100 000 living in these two Nova Scotia towns get to be centenarians.

The happiest Canadians also live in the Maritimes. Research completed in 2007 revealed that Saint John, New Brunswick, was the most livable city in Canada and the happiest Canadians were living there. Quebec City was number two on the happy people/livable cities list, but three other east coast cities — Charlottetown in Prince Edward Island, Moncton in New Brunswick and St. John's in Newfoundland — were ranked third, fourth and fifth.

So if you're looking for a place where you can be happy and grow very old, maybe you should say hello, not farewell, to Nova Scotia or one of the other three Atlantic provinces.

Blue Gold

Maybe people in Nova Scotia eat lots of blueberries. They're supposed to be good for your eyes, your heart, your brain, your colon and various other body parts that start to fail as you grow older, and this province grows a lot of them.

Nova Scotia, along with British Columbia and Quebec, is a world leader in wild blueberry production, and some research shows that wild blueberries are even better for you than cultivated ones.

More and more, people around the world are turning to both kinds of berries as healthy snacks, and blueberry production is booming. By 2007 nearly 227 million kilograms were being produced worldwide. That's a lot of blueberries! By 2008 the small blue berries had become the most valuable fruit crop in Canada.

DID YOU KNOW...

...that Canadian hockey superstar Wayne Gretzky loved playing baseball more than hockey when he was young? He did very well playing shortstop and pitching for local kids' teams in Brantford, and when he was just 10, was quoted as saying, "If I couldn't play hockey, I'd like to play baseball with the Oakland Athletics and [their star pitcher] Vida Blue." But Gretzky could play hockey — wow, could he play hockey — so he did, and baseball's loss was hockey's gain.

IT'S A BIRD?
IT'S A PLANE?
IT'S A MYSTERY

Whatever people observed in the early evening skies above the north coast of Prince Edward Island on December 26, 2007, they were absolutely certain of one thing — they had never seen anything like it before. Two witnesses, Tony and Marie (Ford) Quigley of North Tryon, P.E.I., were driving home when they spotted it, and hurried into the house to get their video camera.

What they watched, and caught on tape, was a small shiny orb moving down slowly — not plunging — from high in the sky, with what looked like dark smoke trailing behind. After a few minutes the object appeared to lengthen and to spiral or twist downward, leaving huge clouds of smoke in its wake. After nearly half an hour, the strange object disappeared from view.

For the next several weeks, the Quigleys tried to find out what they and a few others had watched that night. They showed their tape to reporters, and contacted the local RCMP detachment and officials at the airport in Charlottetown and at Environment Canada. But no one could explain what they had seen. No meteor or comet had flashed across the Maritime skies around dinnertime on December 26, 2007. No secretly launched rocket had exploded, and no piece of space junk had burned up as it fell to Earth.

Eventually the Quigleys accepted the fact that they would probably never know exactly what they had observed. They had joined the ranks of those who report seeing a UFO — an unidentified flying object high in the night sky.

DID YOU KNOW...

...that, according to the UFOlogy Research Centre in Winnipeg, Manitoba, fewer people are reporting seeing flying saucers? Most reported UFOs are still described as being small, round and shiny, but sightings of flying triangles are on the rise.

Research also shows that more UFO sightings are reported in the summer than in the winter. Surprise, surprise. When would most people prefer to stand outside staring at the night sky? Not when the temperature dips below zero, that's for sure.

TV's Reality Comes to Town

The Ruby Café was just to the left of the gas station at the corner of Highway 39 and Grid Road #714. You could stroll past the Dog River Hotel, the offices of The Howler newspaper, and the FOO MAR T grocery store with a D, K and E missing from its sign. If you were looking for a police officer, there was no point going into the police station on Main Street. A tourist might have made that mistake, but local residents wouldn't have. They knew that the building behind the Dog River Municipal Police sign was actually a café called The Stoop, and that the closest real police station was 40 kilometres away from their hometown of Rouleau (not Dog River), Saskatchewan.

For nearly seven years, from 2002 to 2008, Rouleau led a double life. In the real world it was a small town of about 400 people in Saskatchewan, 100 kilometres northwest of Weyburn. In the fictional world of TV sitcoms it was Dog River, a small Saskatchewan town in the middle of nowhere. The words "Dog River" were even painted on the grain elevator, leaving some real-life tourists scratching their heads when they ended up in Rouleau but couldn't find Dog River on a map.

But the award-winning TV comedy Corner Gas, which is set in Dog River, put Rouleau on the map in a big way. Sets depicting the gas station and the Ruby Café were erected, signs saying Dog River were put up on several of the town's buildings, and film crews shot the show's outdoor scenes all around the town. Crowds of tourists showed up each spring and summer, snapping pictures of themselves in front of Dog River's familiar landmarks and hoping for a chance to see the show's stars at work. It's estimated that more than $700 000 flowed into Rouleau because of the show's presence here during its highly successful six-season run.

In 2008 comedian Brent Butt, the creator and co-star of *Corner Gas*, decided he wanted the show to end while it was still enormously popular, and that September the cast and crew finished filming the final season's last episodes. But by then episodes of *Corner Gas* airing in 27 countries were receiving rave reviews, ensuring that the show's presence would continue to be felt in Rouleau.

As long as the town leaves Dog River painted on its grain elevator, tourists from far and wide will still manage to make their way to the little town in the middle of nowhere that isn't marked on any map.

DID YOU KNOW...

...that Brent Butt set his hit show in his home province?

Butt was born and raised in Tisdale, a small town a four-hour drive north of Regina. The two actors who played his character's parents on the show are Saskatchewanians too. Eric Peterson, who played his grumpy dad, Oscar, was born in Indian Head, Saskatchewan, and Janet Wright, Brett's TV mom, Emma, grew up in Saskatoon.

and DID YOU KNOW...

...that *Little Mosque on the Prairie*, another hugely popular Canadian TV sitcom, also took place in a little town in Saskatchewan, in this case a fictional place called Mercy? Like *Corner Gas*, *Little Mosque* became a hit with viewers in more than two dozen countries around the world.

Chilly Dip

On January 19, 2004, Wang Gangyi, a 48-year-old law professor from China, showed up at Bay Bulls, Newfoundland, with a film crew in tow. Wang had come to Newfoundland to honour the memory of the people who died when the *Titanic* sank off the coast of Newfoundland on April 15, 1912. To do so, he threw some memorial wreaths into the icy Atlantic, and then he jumped in after them.

But Wang didn't take a quick in-and-out plunge the way Polar Bear Club folks do each New Year's Day. Oh no. He swam around in the 0.7°C waters for 37 minutes and 30 seconds, another record for China's most famous ice swimmer.

The deadliest...

heat wave in Canada took place in 1936, in the midst of a terrible drought. It gripped the country from July 5 to July 17, claiming the lives of 1180 Canadians.

THeRe's a FiRST Time FOR everything

On August 16, 2008, hundreds of people gathered in Whistler, British Columbia, for the first annual Canadian Cheese Rolling Festival.

Inspired by the famous Cooper's Hill Cheese Rolling races held each May near Gloucester, England, organizers set the course on a long, wide slope with room enough along the sides for spectators to watch the crazy, funny and potentially dangerous event.

On race day many of the participants showed up wearing appropriately cheesy costumes. The smart ones also wore helmets and pads for their knees and elbows. When the racers were lined up at the top of the hill, a special B.C.-made five-kilogram round of cheese was released one second before they took off.

The cheese rolled and bounced down the hill chased by contestants running, stumbling and tumbling after it. But the whole point of the bizarre event wasn't to catch the cheese. The winner was the first person to beat the cheese to the finish line and live to brag about it. And the prize? A five-kilogram wheel of very yummy cheese!

The Little House that Could

In the early hours of July 19, 1996, rain started falling on the Saguenay—Lac-Saint-Jean region of Quebec, north of Quebec City. It poured down all through the night and into the next day, and through to the morning of the 21st. By then as much as 280 millimetres had fallen on the area, producing the worst flood in Canada's history.

Dams burst, dikes failed, and rivers overflowed, spilling torrents of water onto land that was already waterlogged. Sixteen thousand people fled the area as raging rivers gouged out tonnes of mud and rocks, uprooted huge trees, tossed trucks and cars around like bath toys, and washed away entire houses.

But in the midst of the horrific disaster, one little white house in Chicoutimi stood out as a symbol of the people's strength and the region's determination to survive against all odds. Racing water washed away everything around it and surged through its lower floor, but with its foundation built on solid rock, it didn't budge.

Amazing footage of that little house standing firm as
torrents of water surrounded it were part of every
newscast about the disaster airing around the world.
Once the cleanup in Chicoutimi was underway, people
started showing up to stare in awe at the place and to
photograph it.

Years later, people still come to see it. As a waterfall
continues to pour through its front door, it has become
a museum dedicated to recording the story of the worst
flood in Canadian history.

Another House that Could

The flood waters moving toward the home of Jules and Lucy Mourant in the spring of 1997 weren't torrential. They moved silently and steadily, getting higher by the hour. But with the help of more than three dozen friends and strangers, the Mourants had built a four-metre-high wall of sandbags around their house, hoping it would hold back the rapidly rising water heading their way.

The Mourants lived in St. Norbert, Manitoba, a town located along the Red River about a twenty-minute drive south of Winnipeg. And anyone living along the Red River has to at least think about, if not prepare for, the possibility of coping with the river flooding in the spring when the snow and ice begin to melt. A system of dikes, built-up banks, canals, and a 47-kilometre-long channel around Winnipeg is in place to divert the Red's rising waters, but it can't stop it from overflowing.

The spring runoff was especially heavy in April 1997, and the only thing that could have kept the Mourants' house dry was their sandbag dike. And it did! The house was completely surrounded by water for several days, but the Mourants didn't mind being stuck inside. Their home was safe and they were dry.

During the 1997 Red River flood, 28 000 people were evacuated. About 2000 or so cows and 45 000 laying hens were also moved to safety.

The most . . .

snow angels in the world made at the same time were counted up in London, Ontario, in February 2004.

The attempt to break the record for the most snow angels attracted a more bundled-up — and mainly younger — crowd than the one that showed up for the sword fight. Parents and teachers, not just kids, were among the 15 851 folks from 60 London District Catholic School Board schools who all dropped to the ground at once and started swooshing their arms and legs in the snow.

This feat was definitely a record breaker! The previous record — 2282 snow angels made simultaneously at eight schools — had been set by a smiling, rosy-cheeked crowd from the Ottawa-Carleton District School Board on March 7, 2003.

Giant Pumpkins Ride the Waves

The giant pumpkins that farmer Howard Dill started growing in the 1980s put his hometown of Windsor, Nova Scotia, on the map. His monstrous gourds broke four world records and growers from around the world ordered seeds that he bred — Atlantic Giants — to grow their own pumpkins weighing more than 600 kilograms. Windsor also became the place for hopeful farmers from across eastern Canada to bring their orange mammoths each October, to see which one weighs the most.

And in 1999 Windsor became the first place in the world to hold a pumpkin regatta, or boat race. Each year since then, on the same weekend as the weigh-in, crowds of visitors come to Windsor to watch dozens of brave souls struggle to race hollowed-out pumpkins across Pesaquid Lake.

Not everyone makes it across. The veggie boats are very difficult to steer, no matter how hard their owners paddle. They spin and slosh from side to side, and some just tip over and sink. But winning isn't everything. Contestants have as much fun as the spectators at this event, which has become so popular that it's not just the world's first pumpkin regatta — it's also the world's largest.

The largest...
exporter of mustard seed in the world
is Canada.

Canada is the source of 75 to 80 per cent of the world's supply of mustard, and nearly 90 per cent of the mustard seed produced in Canada comes from the province of Saskatchewan. Saskatchewan grows more than 90 per cent of the brown seeds used to make the world-famous Dijon mustard.

Tweet, Tweet

About 80 per cent of the world's supply of canary seed is grown on the Canadian prairies.

Canary seed is a particular type of tall grass that produces seeds covered with a shiny yellow coat, or hull. There's really only one use for canary seed: it's the main ingredient of bird food mixtures. Both caged and wild birds are attracted to its yellow hulls, and they seem to like its taste too.

Kitty Cats Camp Out on Parliament Hill

For as long as anyone can remember, stray cats of all sizes and colours have been hanging out on Parliament Hill in Ottawa. At one time some of them earned their keep chasing after mice inside the Parliament Buildings, but as their numbers increased they became more of a nuisance than the rodents and in 1955 they were evicted.

The cats liked the neighbourhood so they didn't go far. Instead they formed a wild, or feral, cat colony, hunting for their own food and accepting handouts from passersby and outdoor workers. In the 1970s a woman named Irene Desormeaux began bringing them food on a regular basis, and in the 1980s another cat lover named René Chartrand started helping her care for them. But Chartrand didn't just feed the more than two dozen feral felines. He built them little wooden apartments.

In 2008, at 86, Chartrand was still showing up almost every day to feed the 12 or so remaining cats that called his kitty condos home. And as long as there are still cats hanging out on Parliament Hill, volunteers will care for them and tourists will pay them a visit when they check out the Hill.

First-Class Feline Care

A few stray cats that showed up on Parliament Hill have gone to live in far more impressive homes than the wooden structures René Chartrand built.

Every now and then Prime Minister Stephen Harper would take one home to 24 Sussex Drive, the official residence of the leader of Canada's government. There, Mr. Harper and his wife, Laureen, both cat lovers, would give the wild creature extra care and affection until it was comfortable living with humans. Then it could be adopted by someone ready to give it a permanent home.

Mr. Harper also brought home the occasional stray when he and his family lived at Stornoway, the residence of the leader of the official Opposition.

Pricey Panties

On July 30, 2008, Barbara Rusch, a Toronto, Ontario, property manager, bid $9000 by phone on an item being auctioned off thousands of kilometres away in Derby, England, and she was delighted when the auctioneer said, "Sold!"

Rusch had just bought a very expensive pair of underpants that were more than 100 years old. The underpants were large — 110 centimetres wide. They had to be, because their former owner had been a big lady. Rusch was a collector fascinated by the 19th century, and she had just paid $9000 for a pair of Queen Victoria's bloomers.

It's Official

Canada was the first country in the British Commonwealth — even before Great Britain itself — to recognize the position of leader of the Opposition.

The Opposition leader was, and still is, usually the leader of the party with the second-most number of votes. But the job was just traditional, not official, until 1905. That year the Canadian government finally passed a law that made leader of the Opposition an official post with a salary and an allowance covering the expenses needed to do the job. Britain — the model for Canada's government — didn't pass a law like that until 1937.

No Thanks!

Even though Stornoway is a very nice house — a fully furnished mansion worth about $5 million — complete with staff to cook, clean and drive for its official residents, one leader of the Opposition refused to live there.

When the Liberals led by Jean Chrétien won the federal election held in October 1993, the party with the next-highest number of seats was the Bloc Québécois. So the Bloc became the official Opposition and its leader, Lucien Bouchard, became Opposition leader.

Bouchard took the additional pay that comes with the job, but he didn't take Stornoway. Since he was leader of the party that wanted Quebec to become independent of, or separate from, Canada, Bouchard refused to move into a residence owned by Canada and paid for by Canadians. Instead, he found a place to live across the Ottawa River in Hull, Quebec.

Jean Chrétien's Liberals won the election held in June 1997 too, and that time the Reform Party led by Preston Manning won enough seats to become the official Opposition.

Before the election Manning had often complained about government wasting taxpayers' money and giving special bonuses, or perks, to many people on Parliament Hill. So, afraid that he'd look like a phony, right after the election Manning said that he didn't want to move into a mansion. He said it was much too fancy for him and his family. But, after a few weeks, he changed his mind and went along with the tradition of the Opposition leader living rent-free in Stornoway, one of the perks that comes with the job.

Royal Refugees

Before Stornoway became the Opposition leader's official home in 1950, it was home to the first member of a royal family ever to be born in North America. Margriet, the royal baby, was born in Ottawa on January 19, 1943. Her royal mum was Dutch Crown Princess Juliana, who was next in line to become queen of the Netherlands.

Juliana's mother, Queen Wilhelmina, had escaped to England when Nazi Germany invaded the Netherlands in May 1940, and stayed there until World War II ended. But to keep her only child — the heir to the throne — as safe as possible, she sent Juliana and her two children to live in Ottawa with Canada's Governor General until she found a house to rent — Stornoway.

A Royal Thank You

During her stay in Canada, Princess Juliana insisted on living like other Canadians, sending her girls to public schools, shopping for her family's groceries and waiting her turn for service. There was one time when she did get special treatment. That was when baby Margriet was born at the Ottawa Civic Hospital. The rooms where the Princess delivered the baby were declared to be extraterritorial, or outside Canada's control and laws; otherwise, the baby would have been born Canadian, not Dutch — the citizenship of her mother — and wouldn't have been in line to succeed her.

The Dutch royal family moved back to the Netherlands after the war ended in 1945. Back home, Princess Juliana arranged to send Canadians a very special thank-you gift for giving her refuge — 100 000 tulip bulbs to be planted in Ottawa, and another 20 000 each year after that. Juliana became queen in 1948. It is thanks to her Royal Highness that nearly one million tulips bloom in Ottawa each May, when the annual Tulip Festival is held.

The best...

country in the world to see the northern lights is Canada.

Because northern Canada is so close to the North Pole and has such low levels of light pollution, it's the best place to view the spectacularly beautiful aurora borealis.

Oink, Oink

Pigs don't drink tea, they don't water gardens, and they certainly don't take baths. In fact, they do very few things that consume water. On average, one Canadian pig uses just 7 to 8 litres of water a day hanging out on a pig farm. That's how much Canadian humans use just washing their hands under a running tap.

On average, a Canadian uses about 350 litres of water a day, at least fifty times as much as a pig's daily consumption and more than three times as much as a Dane uses in Denmark. Oink, oink ...

What's Cooking?

There was nothing trivial about the Matheson Fire in July 1916. Also known as the Great Fire of 1916, it was Ontario's deadliest forest fire. It claimed at least 240 lives and left hundreds homeless as it roared through more than 202 000 hectares of northern Ontario. At times the front edge of the blaze was nearly 65 kilometres wide, engulfing everything in its path. Several towns north of Timmins, including Matheson, Cochrane, and Iroquois Falls, were reduced to ashes.

But one small group of survivors who had lost
everything discovered an unexpected side effect of
the fire. As they searched for something to eat, they
came across some chickens in a field that had escaped
the flames. The chickens were dead. They were
roasted too. The heat had also cooked potatoes that
had been growing in the field. So, while waiting several
days for help to arrive, the survivors didn't go hungry.
They ate the chickens first, and then dug up, and into,
the baked potatoes.

Polar Bear

Retirement Home

Cochrane, Ontario, was rebuilt after the Great Fire of 1916. Located about 100 kilometres north of Timmins, the town of about 5300 serves as the starting point of an amazing train trip (formerly the Polar Bear Express) that ends 300 kilometres farther north at Moosonee on James Bay. Each summer tourists make the trip in hopes of seeing polar bears in the wild.

But if they miss them in Moosonee, they can still see some up close at the Cochrane Polar Bear Habitat. They can even swim with them there! The Habitat, which opened in 2004, features a large wading pool separated from the bears' enclosure by a super-thick glass wall. When the bears swim up to the see-through wall, waders — especially young ones — on the other side experience the thrilling sensation of sharing the pool with the magnificent snow-white giants.

In southern Ontario, the Toronto Zoo closed its polar bear exhibit in 2007 so that a new and improved one could be built. There was only one bear left at the zoo by then, a 27-year-old female named Bisitek. Near the end of August she was sedated and moved to an excellent new home — the Polar Bear Habitat in Cochrane, where Nikita and Aurora, two other bears from Toronto, were already enjoying their retirement years. The only work expected of them — and her — for the rest of their lives is posing for tourists with cameras.

...that Cochrane, Ontario, is also the hometown of a man whose name is a household word in Canada?

In 1930 Miles Gilbert Horton was born in Cochrane. Nicknamed Tim, he went on to become a star player for the Toronto Maple Leafs. In 1964 he opened his first doughnut and coffee shop.

Cold Comfort

Some world records are far more remarkable than others. But being number one at something ordinary can be fun, as long as it isn't harmful, illegal, or ridiculously dangerous.

Buying, selling and sucking up Slurpees — the frozen, flavoured drinks sold at 7-Eleven stores — is definitely pretty ordinary, but Winnipeggers still think it's fun to be named the Slurpee capital of the world. In 1999, and for the next eight years running, Manitoba's capital earned that title — and a trophy — because a 7-Eleven store in the city sold more Slurpees than any other store in the world. Not only that, in 2007 eight of the top ten Slurpee-selling stores in North America were located in Manitoba.

You might not expect so many people would slurp up so many frozen drinks in a place that's pretty chilly for half the year. But they did. Maybe they suffer from the most brain freezes too.

...that icebergs aren't salty? They float in the ocean but they aren't big pieces of frozen sea water. They're huge chunks of ice that break off the edges of glaciers — massive masses of hard-packed snow that build up on land — and drift out to sea.

So, melted iceberg ice isn't salty. And it isn't polluted either, since it comes from glaciers formed thousands of years ago, long before the air was filled with smog. In fact, it's considered to be some of the most drinkable water in the world. That's why icebergs are being "harvested" in Newfoundland. Large sections are broken off, cut into smaller pieces and melted. Then the iceberg water is marketed as exceptionally pure bottled water, and as a key ingredient of some premium beers and vodkas.

Just the Stats

Ninety per cent of Newfoundland's icebergs calve, or break away from glaciers, along the west coast of Greenland. Icebergs from there travel an average of about seven kilometres per year, making them some of the fastest-moving icebergs in the world.

A Big Cheese

The first cheese factory in Canada was built in Ingersoll in southwestern Ontario. Within a few years it was producing cheddar as fine as any being made in Europe, and by 1866 factory owner James Harris had decided it was time to let the world know just how tasty Oxford County's cheeses were. So he came up with a plan to promote them in a big way — by making a very big cheese.

Harris had no trouble recruiting two other producers
and more than 250 dairy farmers in the area to help him
with his plan. Together they collected the coagulated milk
solids, or curds, from nearly 32 tonnes of milk from 2400
cows. Then Harris supervised the mixing, pressing and
turning of the cheese. After aging for three months, the
huge cheese weighing 3310 kilograms was ready to roll.

In August 1866 townsfolk cheered as Harris had it loaded
on a train bound for a state fair in Saratoga, New York.
It was a huge hit there. People had never seen such a big
cheese. Then Harris shipped the massive cheese off on
a grand tour of England and Europe. After several weeks
travelling from city to city, it was bought by a wholesaler
in Liverpool, England, who cut it up and sold it to small
shops and individual cheese lovers. But a 40-kilogram chunk
was returned to Ingersoll, where one small piece of it is
still on display in the Ingersoll Cheese Factory Museum.

A *Really* Big Cheese

Nearly 30 years after the big cheese from Ingersoll, Ontario, made its debut, one from Perth, Ontario, came along that made it look puny. Known as The Mammoth Cheese from Perth, it was nearly 2 metres high and 8.5 metres around, and weighed in at 9980 kilograms — more than three times heavier than the Ingersoll cheese. One year in the making, it was ready just in time to travel by train on a special flatbed car to the Chicago World Expo in 1893.

The cheese was the talk of the fair, and rightly so: it was the largest cheese in the world. That record stood until 1964, when a round of cheddar from Wisconsin, USA, tipped the scales at 15 853 kilograms at the New York World's Fair.

Perth is still proud of its giant cheese. A piece is proudly displayed at the museum here, and there's even a full-size concrete replica of it near the railway tracks.

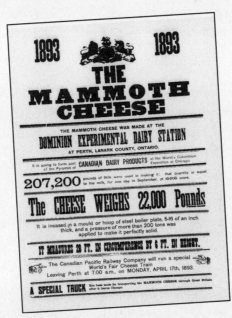

Them's Fightin' Words

Perth, Ontario, holds another place in Canada's history — as the site where the last duel to the death in Canada was fought. It was here that two young law students, Robert Lyon and John Wilson, came face to face early on the morning of June 13, 1833, because of a quarrel over a supposed insult to a young lady in town.

Both men's first shots were misses, so their quarrel should have ended then with a simple apology. But pride and foolishness got the better of them, and they stepped apart and fired their pistols again. This time Wilson's bullet found its mark and Lyon fell to the ground mortally wounded.

At the time no one could have known that that particular duel to the death would be Canada's last. But because it was, the set of pistols Lyon and Wilson used are on display in the Perth Museum.

...that Saskatchewan is the only province with an official sport?

Canada has two official sports — hockey and lacrosse. In 2001 the Saskatchewan government decided to have one too, and voted to give curling that special status because the sport is so popular in the province and to honour the many national, world and Olympic championship performances by star stone throwers from Saskatchewan.

Critter Crossing

Banff National Park in Alberta is the only national park in North America with a major highway — the Trans-Canada Highway — cutting right through it. Tourists and residents appreciate the highway, but for wildlife in the park, it can be a deadly trap.

During the 1980s the road east of Banff was upgraded to a four-lane divided highway. Eleven underpasses were created to provide safe, car-free ways for animals to cross. In the late 1990s the 35-kilometre section of highway west of Banff was expanded too. Another eleven underpasses were built and 2.4-metre-high fences were erected well back from the road. Two new — and very different — overpasses were also constructed, each costing about $1.5 million. They, and all the underpasses, were put in place at key locations where animals were more likely to try to cross the road.

The new overpasses are not meant to carry vehicles. Intended for four-legged pedestrians, they are, in effect, elevated footpaths as wide as football fields. They slope gently upward as they approach the highway, and they're covered with dirt, grass, bushes, shrubs and short trees. The idea is to make them look like hilly extensions of the woods and meadows that border the road. The mounded earth and the shrubs and trees growing along the edges block distant views of the road and form a natural sound barrier that muffles traffic noise.

During the first year that the million-dollar overpasses were in place, just one black bear and one cougar crossed over them. Later, researchers would discover that black bears and cougars prefer using the narrower, more enclosed underpasses. But after a few years, more and more animals, especially grizzly bears, moose, deer, elk and wolves, started using the wide pathways meant to reduce their chances of ending up as roadkill. Now, if people could only come up with road signs the animals could follow . . .

A Grouch's Home Sweet Home

Every town needs one. That's what the residents of Evansburg, Alberta, decided when they erected a sign welcoming visitors. The sign said Evansburg was home to lots of friendly people — and one grouch. The way folks saw it, admitting there was one cranky resident took the pressure off everybody else to be friendly all the time. Just for the fun of it, in 1979 the townspeople voted to select a real live official town grouch, and they've been doing it ever since. The person chosen can be as annoying as he or she dares to be for a whole year. There's also a large wooden Grouch Bench in town where someone feeling grouchy can sit and grumble, but only for one hour. The time limit is clearly displayed on a sign on the bench.

The biggest...

bicycle festival in the world is held every year in Montreal, Quebec, from the end of May through the first few days of June.

Bike lovers from across Canada and around the world join thousands of Montrealers to herald the beginning of summer with Bike Fest, a five-day celebration of cycling. Some people come for the parties and concerts, others for the picnics and family-friendly cycling tours, but almost all of them are there for the Fest's two main events.

About 12 000 riders join in the fun of a *Tour la Nuit* on the Friday night — a 20-kilometre ride, not a race, through downtown streets. With their bike lights on, they look like a river of yellow and red flowing quietly through the darkness. As many as 30 000 people register and line up to take part in the other main event on Sunday, the *Tour de l'Île de Montréal*. It's a 50-kilometre marathon around the island, led out by the serious riders who are followed by the wildest collection of old, new, big and small bikes and riders. The cyclists are there for the fun of it, and so are the cheering crowds that line the route. Ride on!

The largest...

car park in the world is the lot at the West Edmonton Mall in Edmonton, Alberta. It has room for 20 000 cars, vans, SUVs, station wagons and pickup trucks.

Tempting the Tide

A very unusual competitive run is held at Five Islands, Nova Scotia, off the shore of Colchester County on the Bay of Fundy. The "Not Since Moses" Walk and Run takes place the first week of July on the day of the lowest tide of the year. Dick Lemon, a California resident who bought Long Island — one of the Five Islands — in 2003, organized the first event in 2007 as a way of sharing the beauty of his new island paradise, and to raise funds for local organizations. It's also a way to give participants the experience of a lifetime.

There's just one day in the year when the tide is low enough that you can manage to reach Long Island by walking on the ocean floor, and that's the day of the run. But you can't dawdle along the way! Whether you enter the five-kilometre walk or run, or the ten-kilometre run, you have to sign a waiver, or legal form, saying you understand the perils involved in participating. As one section of the form reads:

I am aware that because the tides in the area are extreme (going in one six-hour cycle from virtually no tide to 15 meters of water), getting from the start of the event to its finish must occur within strict nature-set limits.

So far, all brave souls have made it to the finish line without dog-paddling for their lives.

...that each July and August up to 2.5 million shorebirds heading south for their winter migration gather in New Brunswick's Bay of Fundy, the site of the world's highest tides?

They stay at several places along the shore for a few weeks so they can feed and build up strength before setting out on their incredibly long, non-stop flight to South America. Like a busy service centre on a major highway, the bay is a reliable and plentiful source of food for the birds. When the tide is out, the exposed seabed teems with tasty morsels they can snap up and gulp down with very little effort.

The waves of birds landing on the beaches and roosting in the trees at Hopewell Rocks Park later in the summer are an amazing added attraction for tourists coming to see the world-famous tides and Flower Pot Rocks. But visitors are asked not to get so close to the birds that they disturb them and make them waste precious energy they'll need for their big trip.

TIED TIDES

The Bay of Fundy is not the only place in Canada to lay claim to the world's highest tides. In 2002 a measurement taken at the Leaf Basin on the southwest corner of Ungava Bay in northern Quebec recorded a tide one centimetre higher than the 16-metre-high tide in the Guinness Book of World Records at the time. But that measurement was never officially recognized. Since then further measurements reveal that tides in the Minas Basin on the Nova Scotia shore of the Bay of Fundy have reached 17 metres, and that those near the village of Tasiujaq on Leaf Bay can reach 16.8 metres. So, with just a mere 20 centimetres separating these record highs, residents of Tasiujaq feel they're entitled to claim that Ungava Bay is tied with Bay of Fundy when it comes to the world's highest tides. It's definitely a close second!

He's the King of the Castle

Lendrum Place is a quiet residential neighbourhood in southwest Edmonton, Alberta. So the one-storey house with the two-storey castle on top of its attached garage is bound to turn heads when people first see it.

The castle wasn't there when a dentist named Ken Wallace bought the house. But after his two daughters were born, he decided that he'd build them a playroom above the garage. When he started the project in the summer of 1980, he was just thinking that his kids would have a lot of fun playing in a room that looked like a castle. By the time he was done, he had built a major addition to the house complete with turrets, mounted cannons, stained glass windows and an armoured knight standing guard on the roof. Inside he installed a working fireplace and a spiral staircase leading to a large loft-like balcony from which any young Rapunzel could pretend to let down her hair. And over the years he furnished it with antiques he found that fitted in with his castle theme.

Wallace's daughters loved their playroom and, years later, his grandchildren did too. When Wallace retired and moved to warmer Arizona, USA, one of his daughters moved into the house, and her children were thrilled to be able to play in their grandfather's castle whenever they wanted.

Mars on Earth

Space scientists are always on the lookout for new places on Earth where they can conduct experiments to help humans prepare for trips to Mars. In the 1990s a small group of them working with NASA were pleased to find what they thought would be an ideal place to study how humans will explore the red planet when they get there.

It was a polar desert — cold, windy and dry, just like Mars. Its valleys and canyons were similar to those on Mars. Its rocky landscape had been shaped by ice ages long ago, probably just as Mars's landscape had been. It had a large impact crater caused by a high-speeding meteor or comet smashing into the earth, and Mars has many such craters. Even its dirt was reddish, as is the fine layer of iron oxide — rust — that covers much of Mars.

The list of similarities went on and on, and the researchers agreed that they had found a nearly perfect stand-in for Mars — Devon Island, Nunavut, in the high Arctic north of Baffin Island.

...that the Stanley Cup — the National Hockey League's Championship trophy — has become quite the world traveller? Since every player on the winning team is entitled to have it visit his hometown, the Cup has been to hundreds of cities and towns across Canada, the United States and Europe. The Cup has a faithful travelling companion when it's on the move. The Keeper of the Cup, an employee of the Hockey Hall of Fame in Toronto, takes care of it on all its road trips.

Stanley Who?

In April 2006, in hopes of building up interest in hockey in Britain, someone got the bright idea of sending the trophy to the hometown of Lord Stanley of Preston, the Governor General of Canada who donated the silver cup in 1892. Michael Bolt, the Keeper of the Cup, was happy to accept that assignment, but after a day or two in London, England, he wasn't so sure that the trip was going to be a public relations success.

He did attract some attention as he walked, cabbed, and bused the large, shiny, heavy trophy around London, because TV camera crews were following him around, but the presence of the magnificent silver symbol of

Canada's national sport barely raised an eyebrow. Most people had no idea what it was. Many of them didn't know who Lord Stanley was either.

But every now and then, Bolt would hear a shout or a cheer as an amazed tourist from Canada recognized the Cup and wondered what the heck it was doing there.

Making Music
in Montreal

Gail Renard, who grew up in Montreal, Quebec, was 16 when the Beatles' lead singer, John Lennon, and his soon-to-be wife, Yoko Ono, arrived in Montreal in May 1969 for a "bed in" in support of world peace. Lennon and Ono stayed in bed for eight days at the Queen Elizabeth Hotel, giving reporters interviews and receiving other entertainers who wanted the United States to end the war with Vietnam.

Montreal was buzzing with news of John Lennon's presence in the city, and crowds of fans gathered in front of the hotel every day in hopes of seeing their idol. Gail Renard was one of those fans. One night she and a girlfriend managed to sneak up some back stairs and a fire escape, and fool a security guard into letting them into Lennon's suite.

Instead of having them thrown out right away, the pyjama-wearing Lennon chatted with them briefly, then grabbed a piece of thin cardboard and wrote the lyrics to a song on it in black marker. Then, just before the girls left, he handed the card to Renard, telling her it was going to be worth something one day.

The words Lennon had written on the card were for a song that he, Yoko Ono and about four dozen guests crowded into the suite were about to record on June 1, 1969.

Thirty-nine years later, Gail Renard decided to sell her favorite Beatles souvenir. On July 10, 2008, at an auction in London, England, someone paid more than $830 000 for Lennon's handwritten words to "Give Peace a Chance."

A Helping Hand from Canada

In November 1981, Canadarm — a 15-metre-long remotely controlled robotic arm — was first launched into space aboard the space shuttle Columbia. Built by Spar Aerospace Limited of Brampton, Ontario, it was used to pick up and move large objects out of or into the space shuttle. Since then it has been used on shuttles to launch and collect satellites and the giant Hubble space telescope.

In 2001 Canadarm 2, a new and improved version of the Canadarm, was delivered to the International Space Station. While the Canadarm was attached to one end of a space shuttle, the 17.6-metre-long Canadarm 2 can move around the space station on tracks, allowing astronauts or engineers remotely controlling it on Earth to continue building and servicing the station. It can be used to do fairly delicate tasks, but it's also strong enough to move a 105-tonne space shuttle.

And in March 2008, Dextre — another Canadian-made robotic body part — was installed on the space station. Looking somewhat like a headless, legless torso, it can ride the same tracks that Canadarm 2 uses or it can be held by the Canadarm and moved around so that its two very nimble, 3-metre-long arms can do all sorts of jobs in space. The dexterous, or agile, Dextre is also loaded with tools, TV cameras, lights and gripper jaws and, like the Canadarms, can be used by astronauts on the space station or remotely controlled from Earth. Not surprisingly, because it can be attached to Canadarm 2, Dextre is also known as the Canada Hand.

DID YOU KNOW...

...that the first recorded discovery of gold in Canada was made in Quebec in 1846 — at least 10 years before it was discovered in British Columbia? In 1846 (some sources say 1834) a young girl named Clothilde Gilbert was crossing a stream near the Chaudière River, about 80 kilometres south of Quebec City, when she noticed something shiny on the shore — a gold nugget about the size of a small prune. The discovery caused quite a stir at first, but since little else was found beyond that day, Gilbert's lucky find didn't lead to a rush for gold.

The most...

northerly military establishment in the world is the Canadian Forces Station (CFS) located at Alert, Nunavut, at the very top of Ellesmere Island in the Canadian Arctic. CFS Alert is also the most northerly settlement where people live permanently.

In keeping with how far north and isolated Alert is, military personnel posted there for just three to six months at a time jokingly call themselves the "frozen chosen." The station also has a fitting Inuktitut motto, *Inuit Nunangata Ungata*, which translates into English as, "the people of the land beyond the land beyond." Alert really is beyond the beyond. It's 725 kilometres north of the nearest Inuit settlement at Grise Fjord, and 4150 kilometres north of Ottawa.

Butt Out or Else

From 1676 to 1759 it was against the law for Quebecers to smoke on the street. Walking around with tobacco in your pocket was also illegal. The punishment for being caught was a whipping with a cat-o'-nine-tails — nine ropes attached at one end to form a most unpleasant weapon.

The longest . . .

hockey game in the world was played outdoors just east of Edmonton, Alberta, in February 2008.

Brent Sakik, the optometrist who organized the event to raise funds for cancer research, flooded a regulation-size rink in his backyard and lined up needed supplies and volunteers. Then, on February 8, he joined 39 other players ready to brave nose-numbing temperatures for at least a few minutes longer than 240 hours — the world record they were aiming to break.

The two teams of 20 players each kept the game going day and night, with weather ranging from a wind-chilled $-40°C$ to an ice-melting $0°C$, and despite numbed fingers and toes, cramping leg muscles, and blistered heels. Finally, on February 18, with TV cameras rolling and scores of friends and strangers cheering them on, 40 exhausted men played the marathon's final hour — hour number 241 — an hour longer than the existing longest game. They had broken the world record, and had raised more than $300 000 while they did it.

Soft as Silk and Smooth as Satin

On September 8, 2008, a line of elegant models strolled down a runway in Toronto wearing stunning creations from eight of Canada's finest fashion designers. The White Cashmere Collection 2008 was the fifth annual fashion show sponsored by Kruger Products of Canada, and the second such show to feature a special Kruger product. In both 2007 and 2008 all the designers participating in the show had to use sheets of the same "fabric" — Cashmere, Kruger's top-selling toilet tissue.

Hot Potato

In July 2008 Agriculture Canada released the Exploits, a new variety of potato bred in Canada by Kenneth G. Proudfoot, a retired plant-breeding researcher from St. John's, Newfoundland. The creamy-white, tasty Exploits was developed to resist potato wart and virus infections and attacks from golden nematodes, diseases that plague potato-growing efforts in Newfoundland. The breed is fittingly named after the Exploits, the longest river on the island of Newfoundland.

Hard Potato

Maugerville, New Brunswick, has a potato that can resist every wart, virus and bug that tries to attack it. It doesn't sprout eyes or get soft and black in the winter, and it never has to be peeled. It just has to stand tall, wearing a big smile and sporting a top hat, waving at people passing by Harvey's roadside market. Known as Harvey's Big Potato Man, the cheery fellow is made of cement and is six metres tall.

One Banana,
Two Banana,
Three Banana,
Four...

In any other store window, it would have looked like any other banana. But the banana that people walked past in the summer of 2008 was in the window of the Gallery Page and Strange on Granville Street in Halifax, Nova Scotia, and it had a $2500 price tag beside it. So this wasn't just any banana. This banana was art.

Titled "Banana Installation," the display was the creation of Michael Fernandes, an instructor at the Nova Scotia College of Art and Design. He first put a ripe yellow banana on the windowsill on June 13. Then, every day or two, he replaced it with a slightly greener one, until on the last day, July 4, a very green banana lay on the sill. Fernandes ate the bananas he removed, often sharing them with gallery co-owners Victoria Page and Victoria Strange. Only the last banana would go to the buyer, together with daily photos of the window display.

But things didn't go quite as planned. On June 16, when Fernandes showed up at the gallery to replace the banana, he found an apple in its place. Over the weekend, pranksters had stolen the banana, leaving behind a note saying it was a terrorist threat. Fernandes was not amused. And he wasn't too pleased when his creation didn't sell either — although he did get two nibbles. Until gallery owners changed his mind, he had planned to ask $15 000 for it.

...that, at one point in the 1980s, fan interest in the Ottawa Rough Riders Canadian Football League (CFL) team was so low that the players bought 7000 tickets to a home game with their own money?

They figured that giving away the tickets would boost interest and bring the team some good publicity. Maybe it did in the long run. But only 1500 or so fans took them up on their offer of free tickets to that game.

Even the Saskatchewan Roughriders, often called the most-loved team in the CFL, were struggling financially in the 1980s. Before the 1987 season opened, the team's management offered season's tickets to farmers in exchange for a tonne of wheat.

A Test of Fan Loyalty

No matter how long it's been since the Toronto Maple Leafs hockey team won the Stanley Cup, the team's fans stick with them through thick and thin. But on March 19, 1981, 14 years after the Leafs had won their last championship, their loyalty was sadly tested as they suffered through the first period of a game against the Buffalo Sabres. In that period the Sabres scored nine goals, the most ever scored in just one period. But that wasn't the only blow to the Leafs' morale that night. They scored four goals, but by the time the game ended, the Sabres had chalked up *fourteen*, the most goals ever scored against the Leafs in a single game.

Better Late than Never

For as long as he could remember, Lyall Gow, a World War II veteran from Ottawa, Ontario, had wanted to parachute from a plane. So when a friend who was a pilot offered to take him up for a jump, Gow leaped at the chance. He arranged to make the jump strapped to a tandem diving instructor from the Gananoque Sport Parachuting Centre in Gananoque, Ontario, just east of Kingston.

On Saturday, June 28, 2008, Gow showed up at the Centre accompanied by about two dozen family and friends, waving to them as he boarded the plane. Soon the plane was airborne and, not long after, Gow jumped, along with the trainer, experiencing the thrill of free-falling for two minutes before the parachute opened.

After Gow had landed safely, he joked about how he might jump again in five years — when he turned 100. When he made the jump he was nearly 96 years old!

Made to Honour

The first time Canada sent troops into combat overseas was in the fall of 1899. The British government had asked for help fighting the Boers — people of Dutch descent — in South Africa.

More than 7000 Canadians served during the Boer War (1899-1902). The first 1000 arrived in December 1899, in time to be involved in a major battle two months later at Paardeberg, about 1000 kilometres north of Capetown.

Among the many brave men who fought heroically at Paardeberg, one enlisted private — the lowest military rank — stood out for his efforts. On both February 18 and 28, 1900, Private Richard Rowland Thompson risked his own life going to help some wounded comrades. Weeks after the battle, Thompson became so sick that he was sent home to recover.

A woolly scarf followed him to Canada. The gift had arrived for him in South Africa shortly after he had left. During times of war, knitting warm socks, hats, gloves and scarves was one way mothers, wives and daughters of soldiers, sailors and pilots could take care of their loved ones. Thompson's fringed, dull yellow scarf had been crocheted by an 81-year-old woman in England who wanted to show her personal appreciation for the efforts of men like him. The woman was Queen Victoria.

Crocheting eight such scarves just months before she died was the queen of England's way of honouring troops embattled in South Africa. She made four scarves for British soldiers, and one each for "the most distinguished private soldier" from Australia, New Zealand, South Africa and Canada — the four Commonwealth countries that had answered Britain's call for help. Officers who had observed or learned of Thompson's actions at Paardeberg had selected him as Canada's most distinguished private, and the scarf was properly presented to him when it followed him home.

In 1965 the scarf was presented to Canada at a special parliamentary ceremony. It has been proudly displayed at the Canadian War Museum ever since.

A for Effort

On September 15, 2007, more than 500 Boy Scouts from southern Alberta and southeastern British Columbia gathered at the zoo in Calgary, Alberta, in search of a new world record. At the zoo they were joined by a group of students from SAIT (Southern Alberta Institute of Technology) who had brought along two machines they had designed and made specifically for the Scouts.

The record the Scouts wanted to break was for the most popcorn popped in eight hours, and the machines that the engineering and technology students had made were two giant popcorn makers.

The Scouts filled the poppers with kernels and at exactly 8:02 a.m., turned them on. All day long they carted away big buckets of popcorn that the poppers kept popping at a rate of 57 litres a minute. At exactly 4:02 p.m., everybody involved stopped. The number of buckets was totalled and that number was multiplied by the volume of popcorn each one held. The final calculation showed that the Scouts had popped an amazing 34 000 litres — or 34 cubic metres — of exploded kernels.

Unfortunately for the Scouts, the existing record was 48 420 litres — or 48.42 cubic metres. They weren't even close.

Fortunately for the elephants, gorillas and other zoo residents, the popcorn was all theirs to eat.

They Made It!

On July 24, 1988, a much smaller group of Albertans — about two dozen — set out to break another world record. Led by Mike Rogiani, the so-called "ice cream king" of Edmonton, the group filled an empty swimming pool temporarily installed in the West Edmonton Mall with truckloads of 65 different flavours of ice cream and 6 different flavours — butterscotch, strawberry, chocolate, pineapple, caramel and fudge — of sticky, yummy sauces. Then they topped it all off with dozens of litres of whipped cream covered in peanut sprinkles and juicy red cherries.

The ginormous pool of ice cream weighed in at 24.91 tonnes (about 25 000 kilograms), a new world record for an ice cream sundae.

Thousands of spectators showed up that Sunday to see Rogiani's edible masterpiece, and many of them paid $1 for a two-litre pailful. Rogiani and his team of family and friends sold about 5000 pails, with all the sales going to support a children's ward in a local hospital.

It took about four hours to make the sundae. It took about eight hours to clean up afterward.

Walking the Line

Stanstead, Quebec, is a small town about 150 kilometres east of Montreal on the border with the state of Vermont, USA. Derby Line, Vermont, is a small town about 150 kilometres east of Montreal on the border with the province of Quebec, Canada.

But the two towns aren't just close together — they are actually *joined* together in places. They even share certain streets and buildings. In fact, the Haskell Free Library and Opera House, the main building in both towns, was deliberately constructed on the border between them in 1901 to show how well the people could get along.

But the border between Stanstead and Derby Line isn't just the property line between the two towns. The border between them is THE border — the international boundary between Canada and the United States.

For years residents going about their regular business didn't worry too much about which side of the line they were on. They weren't concerned about crossing the border to visit a next-door neighbour, to move around the shared library, or to go in the front door of an apartment building and out the back way. They didn't even think about the fact that the kitchens in some houses were in one country and the dining rooms were in the other. And Americans living on the south side of Canusa Street, which is in Canada, didn't check in with a border guard every time they backed out of their driveways and entered Canada.

But after the terrorist attacks in the United States on September 11, 2001, the American government began doing a lot more to strengthen control of the country's border crossings. Security cameras were installed to monitor the three unguarded streets that cross the border, and sensors were placed in the streets to detect cars driving across. People who did cross had to report what they'd done to American or Canadian border officials at one of three guarded crossings as soon as possible, or they would be tracked down and questioned.

Townsfolk also had to start reporting that they were about to enter or leave Canada or the United States before they crossed certain streets to do their shopping. And since the entrances to the library and theatre are in the United States, if people ever had to run out a back exit in case of an emergency, they'd have to report that border crossing to officials right away too.

Thousands of Bottles of Beer on the Wall

By the early 2000s fewer than two dozen people — mainly artists — were living in Keno City, Yukon, east of Dawson City. A few buildings remain, relics of the years when it was a small, but thriving, mining town. The museum is a must-see for anyone who travels to the end of the Silver Trail highway from Dawson. So is the glass house where Geordie Dobson once lived.

Years after Dobson opened the Keno City Hotel in 1963, he ended up with a huge pile of stubby beer bottles piled up behind the place. Eventually he decided that the time had come to do some serious reusing, and he began building beer bottle walls around the outside of his house. It took Dobson three summers to mortar 32 000 bottles together, but when he was done, he was pleased with the result. Apparently the walls of glass with air trapped inside acted as great insulation.

...that the action-filled movie *Shanghai Noon* (2000), starring Jackie Chan, Owen Wilson and Lucy Liu wasn't filmed in the "wild west" of the American state of Nevada, as the plot indicates? It was filmed in Alberta, mainly in Calgary and the badlands around Drumheller.

The musical hit *Hairspray* (2007), starring John Travolta, Queen Latifah and Michelle Pfeiffer, appears to take place in Baltimore, Maryland. But Toronto and Hamilton, Ontario, stand in for that American city.

The largest...

slab of fudge in the world was made on May 24, 2007, by Chantelle Gorham at the Northwest Fudge Factory in Sudbury, Ontario.

The melt-in-your-mouth blend of cream, butter, sugar, corn syrup and vegetable oil (plus chocolate in part of it) was nearly 14 metres long, 2 metres wide and 10 centimetres thick, and it weighed 2290 kilograms.

A Cookie Monster's Dream Come True

The bag of cookies that went on display at the Loblaws Wonderland Market in London, Ontario, on September 6, 2001, was definitely a shopper stopper. The huge bag made by Loblaws Supermarkets Ltd. stood 3.29 metres high, was 114.3 centimetres wide and 2.13 metres deep. Loaded up with a grand total of 100 152 chewy chocolate chip cookies, it was the biggest bag of cookies in the world.

A Hard Sell

A lot of snow fell around Montreal before Christmas in 2007, so much so that by the middle of December a massive mound two metres high had built up on Michel Levesque's lawn in the suburb of Sainte-Eustache, Quebec. So, just for the heck of it, on December 18 Levesque put up his "magnificent snowbank" for auction on-line on eBay, pointing out that his snow would be perfect for ski hills and warning bidders that there would be no refunds or returns. And he let it be known that he would be sending all the proceeds to a charity called Operation Enfants Soleil that helps children in hospitals.

As Levesque expected, the opening bid was for 99 cents, but the price quickly went up from there, especially after his weird posting on eBay made the news. When the bidding ended, it had reached $3550!

Levesque was disappointed when he found out that the top bid was a hoax. But the next day Sophie Rouillier and Claude Fraser, a couple who had bid the second-highest amount, ended up buying the snowbank for $3000 — and even topping that up with another $550 to match the original false bid.

Levesque was very pleased with how well his wacky idea had paid off, at least from a fundraising point of view. Unfortunately the new owners never arrived to collect their purchase, so he was still stuck with all that snow.

Just the Stats

On average, one half hour spent shovelling snow burns about 410 calories. Raking leaves or washing the car for the same length of time burns about 150 calories and sleeping for 30 minutes will only burn 30 calories. But that means sleeping for eight hours would burn off 480 calories. Hmm... shovelling snow versus sleeping? Nap time!

A Very Long-Distance Call

After working for months on a radio communications project, Patrick Neelin, Paul Je, Kevin Luong and Gino Cunti were ready to demonstrate it. But they weren't sure it would work. At exactly 12:29 p.m. on February 2, 2009, the four students at Humber College in Toronto, Ontario, "handed it in" and held their breath. At that moment, if all went well, the International Space Station would be in position for ten minutes to receive a scheduled message from the radio system they had designed and built themselves.

At first all they heard was static, so they tried to send a second message. And this time, after a few nerve-wracking seconds, American astronaut Sandra Magnus responded from the orbiting station. For the next few minutes, the four young men were able to ask her some technical questions. Magnus, with degrees in electrical engineering and physics, was happy to answer them. She was also happy for the students. As an astronaut who was also a licensed amateur ham radio operator, she understood completely what they had done and why they had wanted to go for it.

Just the Stats

More than 22 000 schools from 164 different countries took part in the two-day-long on-line competition held for World Math Day on March 4-5, 2008. One million students entered. Sixty-five of them were from St. Margaret's Public School in Scarborough, Ontario.

When the math competition ended, six Canadian students were in the top 100. And of those top six Canadians, three came from St. Margaret's. Shourav Saha, who was first in Canada, came 20th in the world. Derek Hawkins was second in Canada and 24th in the world, and Sanan Mujadidi placed sixth in Canada and 76th in the world.

Shourav Saha, first in Canada, was in Grade 5 at St. Margaret's when he entered the competition. During the two days on-line, he had 44 000 right answers, answering correctly about 75 questions a minute!

Photo Credits